Erin Brereton

Illustrations by
Anastacia Zalevskaya

Copyright © 2011 by Erin Brereton

No part of this publication may be reproduced, stored in a retrieval system, or transmitted in any form by any means, electronic, mechanical, photocopying, or otherwise, without the prior written permission of the publisher, Triumph Books, 542 South Dearborn Street, Suite 750, Chicago, Illinois 60605.

Triumph Books and colophon are registered trademarks of Random House, Inc.

This book is available in quantity at special discounts for your group or organization. For further information, contact:

Triumph Books
542 South Dearborn Street
Suite 750
Chicago, Illinois 60605
(312) 939-3330
Fax (312) 663-3557
www.triumphbooks.com

Printed in U.S.A.
ISBN: 978-1-60078-639-6
Design by Andrew Burwell
Illustrations by Anastacia Zalevskaya
Cover design by Paul Petrowsky

TABLE OF CONTENTS

8 Introduction:
GOOD NEWS: YOU'RE A GIRL

10 Chapter 1:
WHY BEING A GIRL IS SO GREAT

☆ First Things First: Just Why Is Being a Girl So Great?

☆ Okay, So I'm Great. Now What?

16 Chapter 2:
GIRLS YESTERDAY, GIRLS TODAY, GIRLS TOMORROW

☆ Movers and Shakers: A Brief Look at Some Culture-Changing Chicas in History

☆ Did You Know?

☆ Femmes and the Future

30 Chapter 3:
BUT ENOUGH ABOUT HISTORY AND LEARNING. LET'S TALK ABOUT PEOPLE WHO REALLY LIKE ME.

☆ The Importance of Having Good Girlfriends

☆ Avoiding Toxic and High-Maintenance Friends

- ☆ How to Be a Good Friend
- ☆ The Importance of Family
- ☆ Your Parents: A User's Guide
- ☆ Family or Friends: Who Wins?
- ☆ How to Be the Awesomest Family Member Ever

56 Chapter 4:
HOW TO HAVE THE PERFECT SOCIAL LIFE

- ☆ School—and Its Social Scene
- ☆ Which Type Are You?
- ☆ Where Do You Fit In? (And Why You Shouldn't Care.)
- ☆ How to Be Outgoing If You're Not Really, Well, Outgoing
- ☆ How to Deal with Bullying (and How Not to Be a Bully Yourself)

70 Chapter 5:
EXCEPTIONALLY AWESOME ENTERTAINING

- ☆ Planning the Perfect Party
- ☆ Party Types and Tips
- ☆ Perfect Party Etiquette

80 Chapter 6:
CLEVER COMMUNICATIONS

☆ Why Your Parents Do Not Understand Why You Want To Text/Call So Much (and How to Avoid Getting Grounded If You Don't Have Unlimited Texting)

☆ When Do You Call, When Do You Click?

☆ Avoiding Texting Disasters and Keeping Stuff Private

☆ Text Abbreviations That Should Exist

☆ Because You Can't Text All the Time

☆ Classic Note-Folding Shapes

100 Chapter 7:
BEING CONFIDENT

☆ Are You?

☆ Confidence: Fake It to Make It

☆ Secrets of Super-Confident People

☆ A Quick Guide to Instantly Upping Your "Wow" Factor

110 Chapter 8:
LIVING A HEALTHY LIFE

☆ How Healthy Are You?

☆ Why You Can't Put Off Living Healthfully

☆ Small Ways to Make Big Changes in Your Health

☆ All About Exercise

122 Chapter 9:
BEAUTYRAMA
- ☆ Your Hair: A Lifelong Struggle
- ☆ Makeup: What You Need to Know
- ☆ Amazing Hair and Makeup Tips
- ☆ And, Of Course, Why Inner Beauty Is the Most Important Thing

138 Chapter 10:
STUDY HABITS OF THE RICH AND FAMOUS (OR, AT LEAST ACADEMICALLY SUCCESSFUL)
- ☆ Five Things You May Be Doing When Studying That Aren't Helping
- ☆ Quick Study Tips That Will Shrink Your Homework Time
- ☆ Avoiding Procrastination (and Stress)
- ☆ Overcommitting

150 Chapter 11:
SETTING (AND REACHING) GOALS
- ☆ Have Realistic Expectations, but Dream Big
- ☆ Setting Goals: How to Get There, Step by Step
- ☆ Your Foolproof Goal-Setting Worksheet

158 Conclusion:
IT'S GOOD TO BE A GIRL

160 About the Author

Introduction: Good News: You're a Girl

Being the best friend ever. Picking out the perfect eye shadow. Getting all your homework done and still having time for dance team practice, four phone calls, and a Skittles break. Nobody said it was easy being a girl.

It is, however, awesome.

Being a boy is fantastic, too— even though they don't have *quite* the same exciting array of shoe or shirt options. They also might not ever get to cry about a horrible day with their best friend and then make it all better by stuffing themselves with Oreos and Diet Dr. Pepper until they think their stomachs are going to explode. Think about it: Boys live their entire lives without using lip gloss even once. You almost have to feel sorry for them.

We girls, on the other hand, can do it all. We can blow $20 at the makeup counter at the mall, spend an hour picking out our outfit, sign up to take a class on advanced math skills, and use our phones until they nearly start smoking from exhaustion—anytime we want to.

Years from now, you might be busy taking care of kids or running from meeting to meeting for your fabulous career—or doing both things at the exact same time. But for now, your job as a girl is just to have fun, learn stuff, and grow up—basically, to find out how to be the best you possible.

You may not know it (and if not, surprise!), but you're on an exciting journey. In the next few years, you'll find out what it means to have really great friends—and how to sort out the people who aren't so great for you.

You'll learn how to drive and become more independent. You'll learn more about history, literature, science, and all kinds of other subjects.

You'll learn about love—and you may even get your heart broken for the first time. (Let's hope not. But if you do, may we recommend cookie dough ice cream to help ease the heartache.)

Most importantly, you'll start figuring out what makes you tick. What kind of things do you like? What don't you like? What makes you feel incredible (cookie dough ice cream)? What makes you feel lousy (running out of cookie dough ice cream)? (I really can't overstress the importance of cookie dough ice cream.)

If you have a ton of questions, don't worry—that's totally normal. That's why we're here: to offer this guide to growing up as painlessly as possible.

This book will walk you through everything you need to know to safely make it to the other side of your teen years. We'll cover everything from study habits to makeup tips to relationship advice. All you need to do is sit back, read, and relax.

Sincerely,

T.R.G.G.T.E. (The Real Girls' Guide to Everything) and Erin (the real girl who wrote it)

Chapter 1:
WHY BEING A GIRL IS SO GREAT

Chapter 1: Why Being a Girl Is So Great

First Things First: Just Why Is Being a Girl So Great?

★ You're good at math, history, English, social studies, geography, and sports; you have great communication skills; and you basically rock at everything else.

★ In fact, more girls are attending college than boys these days. Seventy-five percent of girls plan to attend college immediately after high school, whereas just 61 percent of guys do, according to a recent joint survey from the What Kids Can Do organization and the Lumina Foundation. (Hopefully that means we'll get the nicer dorm rooms.)

★ You always have something to say—and it feels great to say it.

★ Although we're not really sure what goes on at boys' sleepovers (maybe you guys should skip watching TV and fill out some college applications to catch up with our enrollment numbers? *Oooh, burn!*), ours are beyond fun and are frequently filled with candy.

★ You're allowed to wear totally impractical but incredibly adorable shoes with any outfit (even jeans), any time you want to. In fact, it's practically encouraged.

★ Skirts. (Okay, the Scottish may have kilts, but most men never know the joy of wearing a piece of clothing that actually enables you to twirl).

- ☆ Boys are cute, and we get to look at them anytime we want. (Thanks, guys!)

- ☆ You understand that when it comes to fashion, your locker, and life itself, there can never be enough sparkly stuff.

- ☆ You can totally geek out about awesome dresses when you see them in a magazine, or a store, or on your friend (which is really the best scenario because you can borrow it next time you need an awesome dress).

- ☆ "Chick flicks" might be an annoying term, but there's no better way to spend a rainy Saturday afternoon than watching romantic comedies about girls who are klutzy, yet charming.

- ☆ You can play soccer, learn to box, join the track team, and not be criticized for it. (Boys aren't as lucky—they sometimes are ridiculously concerned with being masculine. For example, if a guy wants to take ballet, chances are he may get teased about it. And how unfair is that? We girls understand that what you like to do is what you like to do, end of story.)

- ☆ You understand the *Twilight* series on a different level than boys, teachers, our parents, women over 20...basically everybody on earth.

- ☆ Just because. (Do we really need any reasons?)

Chapter 1: Why Being a Girl Is So Great

Okay, So I'm Great. Now What?

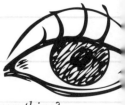

What can you expect from *The Real Girls' Guide to Everything*? Advice. Funny stuff. Facts you didn't know.
Tips so fabulous, you'll wonder how you ever lived without them (we hope).

In the following pages, we're going to take a look at what can we learn from some of the most famous women in history. We'll discuss how important your friends are—how to know which ones are true blue and which are kind of a waste of time—and why your little brother and big sister may be cooler than you think (no, really).

We'll decode boy speak (because let's face it, it truly feels like another language); help you balance work, school, and play; discuss the unspoken rules of texting (like ROTFLYKNTTPITYECL: Rolling on the Floor Letting You Know NOT to Text Personal Information To Your Entire Contact List); and generally discourage you from using blue eye shadow. We'll offer some study tips, help you to lead a healthier life, and talk about how awesome it feels to set— and achieve—a goal.

Basically, we're all about helping you live every day in the most fun, productive, and positive way possible. You should feel great about yourself and everything you do. This book was written to celebrate who you are and all that you can be. You're already fantastic—and with a little help improving things like study habits and self-esteem, you can be even more incredible. Take the advice you like and forget what you don't, but just always remember: we think you're cool.

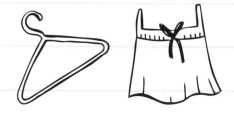

Chapter 2:
GIRLS YESTERDAY, GIRLS TODAY, GIRLS TOMORROW

Chapter 2: Girls Yesterday, Girls Today, Girls Tomorrow

Movers and Shakers: A Brief Look at Some Culture-Changing Chicas in History

Susan B. Anthony

Susan B. Anthony created the National Woman Suffrage Association. Working alongside fellow activist Elizabeth Cady Stanton, Anthony urged the United States government to add a constitutional amendment allowing women to participate in the voting process. (Believe it or not, there was a time when only men could vote.)

In 1872, Anthony tried to vote in an election despite the laws—and was promptly arrested. But she didn't give up. She lectured, collected petition signatures, and toured the country encouraging women to start suffrage movements in their own areas. She fought for the cause until her death in 1906. As a result of her hard work and the work of other suffrage supporters, the 19th Amendment of the Constitution was ratified 14 years later, granting women the right to vote.

Amelia Earhart

In 1928, the world was in a frenzy over the newest technology: aviation. Charles Lindbergh had completed his famous transatlantic flight just a year before; Amelia Earhart took to the skies to prove that a woman could accomplish the same feat. She did—in just 21 hours, becoming an instant celebrity.

In 1935, Earhart became the first person to fly alone across the Pacific by piloting a flight to Oakland, California, from Hawaii—while casually sipping hot chocolate on the plane.

Earhart unfortunately encountered bad luck on her final flight in 1937. Attempting to become the first woman to fly across the world, her plane disappeared over the Pacific. No trace of Earhart was ever found, but she left women with her legacy of courage. "Women must try to do things as men have tried," she once said. "When they fail, their failure must be but a challenge to others."

Marie Curie

Born in Poland in 1867, Curie went to Paris in 1891 to continue her studies at the Sorbonne where she studied physics and mathematical sciences. She followed her husband, Pierre Curie, as head of the Sorbonne's physics laboratory; in 1903, she received her Doctor of Science degree. In 1896, radioactivity was discovered by scientist Henri Becquerel; the Curies in response conducted research to discover the isolation of polonium and radium. Marie Curie's research led to some new ways to use radium's therapeutic elements. For their work, Curie and her husband were awarded half of the Nobel Prize for physics in 1903; Becquerel was given the other half. Curie received a second Nobel Prize in 1911 in chemistry for her work with radioactivity. After her husband's death, Curie became the first woman to be named Professor of General Physics in the Faculty of Sciences. In 1914, Curie became director of the Curie Laboratory in the Radium Institute of the University of Paris, founded the same year.

Chapter 2: Girls Yesterday, Girls Today, Girls Tomorrow

Hillary Clinton

Hillary Rodham Clinton has been a first lady (thanks to her husband, President Bill Clinton); U.S. Senator (the first female senator for the state of New York); the first-ever female presidential nominee for a major party (the Democratic Party); and U.S. Secretary of State (one of three females to ever hold the position).

As the acting Secretary of State, she travels across the world encouraging positive international relations.

Harriet Tubman

Harriet Tubman escaped slavery in 1849 at age 29 by fleeing from a slavery-supporting state to Pennsylvania. Despite the danger of being caught and punished—at one time there was a $40,000 reward for Tubman's capture—she bravely returned to the South repeatedly, leading 300 slaves to freedom in the North through the Underground Railroad.

Rosa Parks

Rosa Parks became a symbol of the civil rights movement in 1955 when she bravely refused to move from her seat on a Montgomery, Alabama, bus in order to make room for a white passenger.

Parks was arrested; in response, Reverend Martin Luther King Jr. quickly mobilized a 381-day boycott of the bus system in Montgomery. The boycott fueled the civil rights movement. In 1964, Congress passed the Civil Rights Act, which helped outlaw racial discrimination in public places.

Josephine Baker

Dancer, singer—and undercover French Resistance operative: Josephine Baker played all three roles during her career. A creative performer, Baker gained fame in the U.S. during the Jazz Age. In addition to performing, Baker also was a sub-lieutenant in the Women's Auxiliary of the French Air Force. Baker used her travels to entertain French and American troops as a cover to help deliver military intelligence reports (some written in invisible ink on her sheet music—how clever is that?). Later in the U.S., Baker extended her political activism by declining to perform for segregated audiences in support of civil rights. For her war efforts, Baker was given the Croix de Guerre and the Medal of the French Resistance with Rosette and was the first American woman to be buried on French soil with military honors.

Anne Bradstreet

Puritan Anne Bradstreet endured a difficult voyage from England to the U.S. in the 1600s; upon arriving in the new world, conditions were also harsh, and Bradstreet's family and cohorts struggled to keep their colony alive. Turning to reading and poetry to cope with the difficulties of daily life, Bradstreet became one of the first poets in the U.S. to publish a work written in British verse when her first collection, "The Tenth Muse Lately Sprung Up in America, By a Gentlewoman of Those Parts," was published in 1650 after her brother submitted it without her knowledge.

Jackie Joyner-Kersee

Jackie Joyner-Kersee was born into adversity in East St. Louis, Illinois, in 1962 and became of the most respected and talented athletes of her generation. Her basketball, volleyball, and track talents were evident in her youth, and she attended the University of California at Los Angeles on an athletic scholarship.

Chapter 2: Girls Yesterday, Girls Today, Girls Tomorrow

She participated in four Olympic Games, won three gold medals (six overall), and set a new women's record for the heptathlon. In 2000, *Sports Illustrated* voted her the greatest female athlete of the 20th century.

Elizabeth Blackwell

Born in 1821 in England, Elizabeth Blackwell was the first American woman to receive a medical degree. Blackwell didn't want to be limited to the small number of career options available in her day, so, while working as a teacher in Kentucky, she decided to become a doctor. Although medical schools were fairly new—most medical students learned their craft by interning with a doctor—Blackwell pored over medical books in her off hours and applied to several. She was rejected from all Philadelphia schools and from schools in New York City and New England. However, after finally being accepted at Geneva College in New York, Blackwell moved to attend classes. The transition wasn't an easy one. She had to sit separately during class; Blackwell was often sometimes barred from educational lab work. Yet in 1849, Blackwell graduated—ranking first in her class—as the first woman to receive a medical degree in the world. During her career, Blackwell published books, helped start the National Health Society, and built what is now called the New York Downtown Hospital.

Katharine Graham

When Katharine Graham's husband, who worked as the publisher of the *Washington Post*, died in 1963, she began working as the newspaper's president. She became publisher in 1969 and pushed her staff to produce more news articles about the Vietnam War and the Nixon presidency.

Under Graham's watch, the paper reached new heights investigative reporting, including publishing the government's top secret "Pentagon Papers"—which included information about the Vietnam War—and Bob Woodward and Carl Bernstein's famed Watergate investigation.

Graham continued to work in the media—as CEO and board chairperson of the Washington Post Company, which owns newspapers, magazines, and television stations—until her death in 2001. She remains one of the most respected women in the journalism industry.

Mary Pickford

By age 15, actress Mary Pickford had already made her Broadway debut; two years later, in 1909, Pickford began appearing in motion pictures—which were still a new art form back then—quickly gaining recognition and eventually becoming one of the most popular actresses in the world. Appearing in more than 130 films, Pickford was making $150,000 a year, during an era where the average annual family income was less than $2,000. In 1916, she signed a deal with Adolph Zukor's Famous Players Film Company to become Zukor's partner. The contract established the Pickford Film Corporation, which produced Pickford's films. The actress also negotiated an admirable salary for her two-year contract: a

Chapter 2: Girls Yesterday, Girls Today, Girls Tomorrow

minimum of $1 million. By 1921, she'd gained even more control, producing, directing and acting some of her movies. She also helped found the Motion Picture Academy of Arts and Sciences and the Oscar awards, winning an honorary Oscar in 1976, three years before her death.

Betty Friedan

Writer Betty Friedan helped articulate a growing sense of alienation felt by many suburban housewives in the 1950s and '60s—and her findings gave birth to a movement.

Friedan first began to realize women's dissatisfaction when she conducted a survey at her 15-year college reunion. She spent the next five years researching economics, sociology, psychology, and history and talking with women. Many were frustrated that the freedom they gained during the career-minded era of the 1920s and '30s had seemed to slip away as women moved into standard roles as housewives and mothers in the 1950s.

Friedan published those findings in her 1963 book *The Feminine Mystique*, which is commonly held to be one of the key nonfiction works of the 20th century and the catalyst for the feminist movement. She also co-founded the National Organization for Women in 1966.

Jane Addams

In 1889, Jane Addams founded Hull House, sponsoring projects to end child labor, improve women's working conditions, and offer educational opportunities for women and immigrants in an industrial, impoverished area of Chicago. Hull House was a huge part of the Progressive Era social reforms and provided a huge career boost for women of the time by helping to encourage women's careers in field like social work and nursing.

However, Hull House wasn't Addams' only career achievement. She also worked as a peace activist during World War I and received a Nobel Peace Prize in 1931.

Oprah Winfrey

One of the most recognizable women in America, Oprah Winfrey was the youngest person (and first African-American woman) to anchor the news at Nashville's WTVF-TV, at age 19. After working in broadcasting in Baltimore, Winfrey moved to Chicago to host WLS-TV's morning talk show *AM Chicago* in 1984.

A year later, the show was renamed *The Oprah Winfrey Show*, and in 1986 it became nationally syndicated. For 24 consecutive seasons, her show has been the No. 1 talk show in America, and is watched by approximately 42 million viewers in the U.S. alone. In 2011, Winfrey launched a new media venture: OWN, the Oprah Winfrey Network. The channel broadcasts to 80 million homes.

Did You Know?

Life for girls today is way different than it was 100 years ago, or even 50 years ago. Your grandmother probably drove a car, but did her grandmother? Maybe not. Things have changed a lot in the past century. (We think for the better!)

Chapter 2: Girls Yesterday, Girls Today, Girls Tomorrow

For example, did you know that 100 years ago...

☆ **Most women didn't have a job in an office or other workplace.** It sounds crazy, but it's true. Only 19 percent of women who were working age (16 or older) were in the workforce in 1900, according to the Bureau of Labor Statistics.

☆ **More women entered the workforce between 1900 and 1920.** The amount of women in the workforce grew during that 20-year period by about two-thirds, from 5 million to more than 8 million, according to U.S. Census Bureau data.

☆ **And only a few of the women who did work were lawyers or doctors.** Just 1 percent of the attorneys in the U.S. were women in 1900; just 6 percent of physicians were female, according to the Bureau of Labor Statistics.

☆ **Many instead worked as a full-time mom.** In 1900, 80 percent of American kids had a stay-at-home mother.

☆ **Being a stay-at-home mom was risky.** Women didn't often know much about prenatal care, and delivery methods weren't as advanced as they are today. Early in the century, six to nine U.S. women died of pregnancy-related complications for each 1,000 live births, according to the Centers for Disease Control and Prevention.

☆ **Thankfully, that's pretty rare these days.** Having a baby is much, much safer! In 1997, out of all the women giving birth in the U.S., only 327 died due to childbirth-related issues.

And in the past 50 years...

- **New inventions helped women have more time to themselves—and more time for their career.** A new flurry of products created in the 20th century (including the refrigerator, washing machine, dryer, microwave oven, toaster, and my personal favorite, the dishwasher) helped homemakers spend less time doing chores and more time taking on paid jobs, according to the Bureau of Labor Statistics.

- **More women started working.** By 1950, roughly one in three women participated in the labor force. (Hizzah!)

- **By 1998, considerably more women had started working.** Sixty percent of women were part of the labor force. (Another reason for the change: Many women had entered the workforce during World War II to fill jobs left empty by men who had joined the armed forces.)

- **More women pursued higher education.** As education and higher learning became more popular, more women went to college—and, as a result, earned more. Women with

Chapter 2: Girls Yesterday, Girls Today, Girls Tomorrow

college degrees earned 65 percent more in terms of hourly compensation than ones with a high school education did by the last five years of the century, according to the Bureau of Labor Statistics.

☆ **Women began getting married later.** And men did, too. Today, the median age at which women get married at is 26, according to the U.S. Census Bureau; men get married at 27. Just 25 years ago, women got married on average at 21 and men got married at 23.

☆ **Less women are full-time caregivers.** By 1999, only 24 percent were full-time stay-at-home moms, according to the Bureau of Labor Statistics.

☆ **More women had become doctors and lawyers.** In fact, by 1999, 29 percent of the lawyers in the U.S. were women, and 24 percent of the nation's doctors were women, according to the Bureau of Labor Statistics.

☆ **Women have started to close the gap between what men and women earn.** In 1979, women earned only 62 percent as much as men, according to the Bureau of Labor Statistics. By 2008, women who worked full time earned a median amount of $638 per week, 80 percent of what men were paid.

The top profession for working women? Management, professional, and related occupations (like bosses, doctors and lawyers). In 2008, 26,813 women were employed in that line of work, according to the Bureau of Labor Statistics.

Less popular: construction, production, or transportation occupations (like builders, factory workers, and truck drivers). Just over 1,300 women were in transportation and material moving occupations.

Femmes and the Future

What Social and Political Achievements Could Be In Store for Today's Girls? (Ahem, the Presidency!)

In the past 100 years women have flown around the globe, become active in politics, and joined the workforce en masse. What's next?

Absolutely anything. That's the exciting part of looking back at the last century. In the past 50 years alone, women have become CEOs of huge corporations, they've flown to outer space, and they've ascended to some of the highest offices in the government.

So what's next? Whatever we want to do and be. That's the great part of looking back at the past—and moving forward.

What do you want to be? An actress? A senator? A fashion designer/celebrity/teacher/writer/chef/physicist/softball star? Any of those career choices deserve a big "You go, girl"—because the future is whatever you make of it.

Chapter 3:
BUT ENOUGH ABOUT HISTORY AND LEARNING. LET'S TALK ABOUT PEOPLE WHO REALLY LIKE ME.

Chapter 3: But Enough About History and Learning. Let's Talk About People Who Really Like Me.

The Importance of Having Good Girlfriends

Aristotle once said that "friendship is a single soul dwelling in two bodies." And if you've ever had a best friend who knew what you were about to say or do before you even did it, you know exactly what that zany Greek philosopher was talking about. (I don't usually advise listening to people wearing togas or other large, sheet-like materials—even with the recent popularity of the Snuggie—but really, Aristotle knew what he was talking about.)

After all, your girlfriends play a *huge* role in your life. Super big. Massive. Immeasurable. Huge times infinity.

I had the same three best friends from 5th grade to senior year. We are, in fact, still friends. They knew every food I hated, every song I loved, every boy I had a crush on (at times, a scroll-like list), and every secret I had. That was VIP information, culled from years of late-night phone chats, passed notes, conversations sitting in cars in someone's driveway at the end of the night, and, of course, big, dramatic announcements. (I have always been a fan of big, dramatic announcements. Here's one to prove it, complete with big, dramatic punctuation: YOUR FRIENDS. ARE SO. IMPORTANT. TO YOUR MENTAL WELL-BEING AND HEALTH!)

Don't believe me? Just ask Sharyl Toscano, PhD, RN, FNP, of the University of Vermont's College of Nursing and Health Sciences. She did a study in 2007 about teen dating and found that girls who had a solid group of friends actually dated more safely and avoided more boyfriend-related abuse.

Toscano found that many of the girls she spoke to dated guys but also socialized with them while hanging with their friends, creating a circle of friends. The girls who withdrew from their social group when dating a guy put themselves in more dangerous situations—not just because they were physically alone, but because they were missing out on all that advice, support, and companionship. Makes sense, right? And it brings a whole new meaning to that old "I've got your back" notion. Because really, in order to have a friend do that, you can't *turn* your back on them. Bad idea.

Another Bonus: Friends Can Help You Stay Happy

Having a good group of friends can also have a huge impact on your day-to-day feelings. Yes, hormones can (and will) wreak their havoc on your moods as you eke your way toward 18. Yes, you will cry at ridiculous commercials. You'll feel moments of fury when your teacher announces a pop quiz you weren't expecting. That's all normal. (Partially because pop quizzes are

Chapter 3: But Enough About History and Learning. Let's Talk About People Who Really Like Me.

really unfair. Nobody wins if the entire class fails because they didn't know to study, Mrs. Charles.)

Some life-related stress is normal. Two weeks of extended sorrow and lethargy? That's depression. And, according to the Substance Abuse and Mental Health Services Administration, 13 percent of girls have experienced that kind of episode in the past year.

A study by the administration found that more girls than boys experienced depression—only 4.6 percent of guys reported depression-like symptoms—and one major effect was girls withdrawing from their social circles. Think about it: it's such a defeating cycle. You get depressed, so you pull away from the people who love you—which only makes you feel more lonely and isolated.

Friends can have a big influence—positive or negative—on your life. According to the Institute for Youth Development, teens who participated in its focus groups acknowledged that friends influence their perception of what's cool, what's trendy—and even whether they feel good or bad on a given day.

That's why it's important to hang out with positive, fun, supportive people. That toxic friend who's always in a bad mood and hates everybody? Hanging out with her can be a downer. But that friend who cracks you up every time she calls? She's probably your first choice for a day shopping or catching a movie.

Remember, choosing your friends—and making all kinds of choices regarding what you do and who you do it with—is absolutely, 100 percent under your control. But how do you know which friends are good friends, and which are always dragging your mood down? How do you balance friends, school, and dating? And how does your family fit into all of this when you start to feel like your friends *are* your family?

Don't worry—it's all easier than you think. And we'll offer plenty of helpful tips on how to weed out the whacked out friends, balance family and friend time, and more in this chapter.

> **Lucky Enough To Have Some Great Friends? Let's Make A Holiday Out Of It**
> National Friendship Day is the first Sunday in August (Aug. 7, this year). If you don't want to shell out for a card or gift, a hand-written note is a great way to tell your buddies they're the best!

Chapter 3: But Enough About History and Learning. Let's Talk About People Who Really Like Me.

Avoiding Toxic and High-Maintenance Friends

Fantastic friends bring a lot of great things to your life: companionship, camaraderie, support, and a lot of warm, fuzzy feelings.

When you think about it, having a good friend is kind of like having a kitten—if kittens could tell you you're great, make you laugh when you're having bad day, and send you funny text messages. (Kittens actually can show affection. Yet due to their lack of opposable thumbs, can't text. Thanks for *nothing*, Mother Nature.)

However, as great as friends are, you may at some point discover that you have one (or maybe more than one) who just isn't bringing much joy into your life. Oftentimes it's someone you've known for a while, but things have just changed. Maybe you've just grown apart or gone down different paths. Sometimes it's a new friend who seemed great at first—but then things got funky.

A toxic friendship—much like a toxic substance—is not something you want in your life.

"Every friendship is difficult from time to time," said Harriet S. Mosatche, PhD, author of *Where Should I Sit at Lunch?: The Ultimate 24/7 Guide to Surviving the High School Years*. "But a friendship that has become toxic is one in which the balance has shifted so that the frustrations, resentments, and disappointments far outweigh the positives."

It's fairly easy to spot an encouraging, equal friendship. "A positive friendship makes you feel good about yourself," said Mosatche. "This kind of friendship is balanced, so that each person receives as much as she gives."

But how can you tell if your friend isn't just having a bad week? "If something is really wrong, you'll know," Mosatche said. "Girls need to learn to trust their gut that something about the relationship doesn't feel right." I believe in cutting friends slack for having a rough day every once in a while. However, I've found that if the bad behavior becomes a consistent situation, the friendship usually starts to feel more frustrating than fun.

Another major sign: Mom and Dad often don't dig your toxic friends. "Parents don't complain about positive friendships, so that's another clue to girls that she's picking appropriate friends," Mosatche said.

Okay, so you've discovered that you have a toxic friend. Now what? The first step is to assess whether or not that friend is someone you really want to keep in your life.

Chapter 3: But Enough About History and Learning. Let's Talk About People Who Really Like Me.

If the friend is someone you've known since kindergarten and has always been a great person to be around—even-tempered, supportive of your goals, and just generally fun—then maybe it's a temporary situation, due to something going on in her life. Are her parents going through a difficult divorce? Did she just get a heinous grade? Is she stressed about a big upcoming game?

If that's the case, your friend may just be temporarily toxic. It may help to ask her if she wants to discuss what's on her mind. "If the friendship is one that a girl really wants to hold on to, she might try talking with her friend about the issues or behaviors that are hurting their relationship," Mosatche said.

However, if bad behavior has been a pattern with this friend for as long as you've known her—or her behavior is downright mean—it's time to question whether or not that girl deserves to be your buddy. Keeping a toxic friend in your life isn't just a hassle; it can affect how you feel about yourself.

Occasionally worrying about your friend group accepting you is normal, according to psychologist Catherine Angelastro. However, a toxic friend can make you somewhat paranoid—which is no good.

"Maintaining that status can cause significant stress and self-confidence issues," Angelastro says.

Nobody needs that kind of pressure! Ask yourself: Is keeping this friend in my life really worth all the drama? Maybe not.

"Often, the best course of action when a friendship has turned toxic is to end it, since this kind of relationship can erode self-confidence

and lead to poor decision-making," Mosatche said.

If you decide to ditch that toxic friend but you're comfortable talking to her about your feelings and trying to improve things first, make sure you're honest but not accusatory.

After all, getting her defenses up won't make the situation better. Just remember that while you have the right to express your feelings, she has feelings, too. (Using statements based on your take on things—like saying, "I felt badly when you didn't call me back" instead of "You should've called me back" can help get your point across without sounding accusatory.)

Another option is to slowly start spending less time together. This can be a low-key way to phase someone negative out of your life. (It's much more subtle than starting a big fight and/or decorating your locker with a "CHRISTINE NOT ALLOWED; FRIENDSHIP IS OVER" sign.)

If you're trying to reduce your interactions with a toxic friend, it may help to spend more time focusing on the truly awesome friends you have in your life. Chances are, you have more than one fantastic, loyal, fun friend! Take a moment and tell that person how you feel. People never get tired of hearing compliments. And by the way, you're amazing, I don't know how you balance everything, but you're doing a great job, so keep up the good work. (See?)

How to Be a Good Friend

Chapter 3: But Enough About History and Learning. Let's Talk About People Who Really Like Me.

You now realize that *having* good friends is important. But how can you be a good friend?

Easy: Just be honest, friendly, courteous, and kind. (And obviously, no cyberbullying. That's mean.)

If it all sounds super simple, it is. But when you have friends from different groups, things can get tricky. "Girls tend to categorize their friendships like they do with eye makeup or school clothes vs. party clothes," Angelastro said. "It's simple enough to say, these are my good friends, my hockey friends, my friends from childhood."

Girls often label different friends to make it mentally easier for them to comprehend how the friends fit into their life, according to Angelastro. "It keeps things easier for different groups to fit into the appropriate bucket," she said.

However, although it may be easier in terms of categorization, merging those different groups—or balancing time with each—can prove challenging. "Lines get drawn, and being friends with all is certainly possible—but managing time with all groups becomes difficult," Angelastro said.

Girls who are involved in a kabillion afterschool sports, clubs, and extra lessons and classes know exactly what she's talking about. "For the most part, young girls are involved in an array of activities, from school-related to religious programs to outside activities, a sports team in school and then a travel team," Angelastro said. "Time management alone then becomes a stressor aside from friendships."

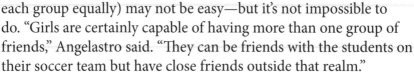

Organizing those various friend groups (and treating each group equally) may not be easy—but it's not impossible to do. "Girls are certainly capable of having more than one group of friends," Angelastro said. "They can be friends with the students on their soccer team but have close friends outside that realm."

One key factor in successfully managing different groups? Being careful not to label things *too* much. (Friends aren't e-mail messages—each one doesn't need to be put in a specific folder.)

It's totally fine to sometimes invite your volleyball friends out with your National Honor Society friends. (Although probably not to play volleyball—because the friends who play it every week would probably easily win.)

Just be careful about what terms you use to describe your various friend groups. "Most of the students I have seen successfully balance these groups refer to them as 'my friends' and then 'my

Chapter 3: But Enough About History and Learning. Let's Talk About People Who Really Like Me.

close friends,'" Angelastro said. "It is always important for tweens to consider how they would like to be treated. Would they want to feel embarrassed or left out?"

Ignoring a close confidant or purposefully leaving her out of fun plans because you don't think she'd fit in with your other friends could make her think you're a toxic friend because you were trying to keep things separate.

"It's impossible to guarantee that girls will never act in toxic ways," Mosatche said. "But [ask yourself] questions, such as, 'How do you think that made her feel?'"

Trying to understand where the other person is coming from can help you settle—or avoid—a lot of conflict.

"The more empathic girls are, the less likely it is that they will do or say hurtful things to their friends," Mosatche said. "And if the friendship is a deep and honest one, friends will be able to frankly tell each other when one is beginning to act in selfish ways."

The Importance of Family

You love them, you're annoyed by them, they made you. They're your parents. And while they can be a wonderful source of support (and let's be honest, cash when you really want new clothes), they can also seriously. Get. Under. Your. Skin.

Why is that, anyway? I mean, it seems like they have the best of intentions. They love you. They want you to be happy and safe. They want you to make the right decisions. And they also want

you to clean your room.
Riiiiiiight. That's where it gets sticky. (Hopefully not literally. If part of your room is actually sticky, that's a clear sign that it really does need to be cleaned right away. But

pants on the floor? Totally not something mom needs to freak out about. Just tell her that it's a decorating choice.)

As you get older, you may find that your parents play a different role in your life. You used to come home from school and confess all the details of your day to your mom over brownies and soda. Chances are your best friend now gets more detail during your nightly text session (or during one of several nightly text sessions).

It's not that you no longer like brownies. (Why wouldn't you? They're delicious.) And it's not that you don't want your mom to be part of your life anymore. (Particularly when you have a lot of laundry. Moms have a magical way of washing, drying, and ironing things to make them look brand new.) But suddenly, it seems like your world has shrunk to include your best friends at the center, and your parents somewhere way on the outside of all that.

Which—according Mosatche—is totally normal.

Chapter 3: But Enough About History and Learning. Let's Talk About People Who Really Like Me.

"As girls work on becoming more independent from their parents, friends take on increasingly important roles as confidants," Mosatche said.

Mom and Dad don't disappear completely, but they do take a back seat.

"Girls still depend on their parents for guidance and continue to need the love and support parents provide," Mosatche said. "However, teen girls need to begin to separate, both physically and emotionally, from their parents."

In other words, it's part of the process of growing up (which, whether you and/or your parents like or not, is going to happen).

So even if your mom's stuck with a few extra brownies and a little less conversation time, it's not something she should feel bad about. "Making meaningful relationships outside the family is a clear sign of positive development, and parents should encourage that," Mosatche said.

That doesn't mean your family has no importance anymore—you can't discredit the value of people who love you unconditionally and always have your best interests in mind. They love you. You love them. And that's a fantastic thing. As you get older, chances are, you'll circle back around and grow closer—even if, in middle/junior high and high school, you tend to spend more time with your at-school social circle than with the 'rents.

So go ahead, confide in your friends. Make some new ones. Keep a journal for self-reflection. But also clean up that sticky thing in your room. Trust me: If you're looking for roommates, jam and marshmallow fluff are *not* your best options.

Your Parents: A User's Guide

Your friends may feel like your family right now. After all, you spend most of your time each day with them, they know all your secrets, you tell them *everything*.

However, with your parents, sometimes it just feels like they just don't get your life and what you're going through. Sure, they were teenagers once (allegedly). You've seen the photos. That hair, those clothes, that ridiculous music they sometimes play as they reminisce about how it "takes them back." Could that be ANY more different than your life?

Unless you like neon, tiny backpacks, flipped up collars, giant hair, or any of the other zany, oddly vibrant things your parents wore when they were your age, then probably not. However, chances are that when they were teenagers, they felt as if their parents didn't understand them either. (Even if that technically was back before

Chapter 3: But Enough About History and Learning. Let's Talk About People Who Really Like Me.

the earth cooled and became a planet.)

Many teenagers feel like they're living in their own little world—and in a way, they are. It's called "school," there's a gym requirement, and the food is absolutely awful.

Getting closer to friends—and bonding less with your folks—is part of getting older. And according to Mosatche, it's not necessarily a bad thing.

"Friendships allow girls to try out different ways to relate to people who are not family members," she said. "Even more important, these relationships provide validation for the concerns and feelings that girls are experiencing."

Exactly! Because your best friend knows just what it feels like to have a crush on someone who doesn't even seem to know you exist. (Although he probably does know that you exist. Guys can be surprisingly shy, too.)

Your best friend knows how unbelievably stressful this week is going to be for you because she's sweating out those after school rehearsals and quizzes, too. You're in the same boat—and it's the S.S. *Teenager*. Your parents? They're not even on the dock to get into the boat (which is, of course, covered in driver's licenses, sparkly eye shadow, and varsity jackets, and is helmed by two of the Jonas Brothers).

You may feel a growing distance between you and your parents. Just remember that if you feel it, they probably do, too. Pulling away from your parents can make you feel both independent and guilty. Which is the right feeling? And even if you know pulling away is part of growing up, how do you do it without hurting anyone's feelings?

As in any situation like this—whether you're breaking up with a boyfriend, upset with a friend over something she did, or frustrated with a co-worker—being honest and open is the best policy. If you sense that your mom feels shut out of your life—or you feel like she's, say, reading your diary when you're at school (which I'm pretty sure mine did for a while—until she realized my teenage rebellion involved getting my ears double-pierced and stopped reading out of boredom), then speak up.

When it comes to any relationship—including the one with your parents—communication is key.

"Respect, honesty, and love are the key ingredients in a positive relationship," Mosatche said. "Teens and their parents can and will disagree, but it's how they express those feelings that hurts or enhances the relationship."

Don't expect your mom to be your friend. It's more important that she's a role model to you, according to psychologist Catherine Angelastro, who has worked as a school crisis counselor and the director of guidance at two schools in New Jersey.

So understand that your mom (and dad) may have to make decisions that you might not agree with or like.

Chapter 3: But Enough About History and Learning. Let's Talk About People Who Really Like Me.

Your parents' job isn't just to be your friend. Even so, if you have something to say or you are upset about something, it's always okay to talk to your mom about it. You never know—she may have gone through the exact same thing when she was your age (in 6 B.C).

"Reach out to your mom," Angelastro said. "She's been training for this her whole life."

It also doesn't hurt to plan in some family time to keep the 'rents (*and* you) happy.

While your parents' work schedules and your crazy afterschool calendar may mean you can't do dinner every night, Mosatche suggests scheduling one family meal a week as a way to reconnect. Or try taking a family field trip.

"Doing something fun together once in a while also reminds everyone how important families are," she said.

So don't make any plans to skip out on Thanksgiving dinner or get your own apartment just yet—because it really is important to still have some family interaction.

Family or Friends: Who Wins?

When you've got a crazy schedule and some seriously fun friends who are always ready to hang out, it's easy to make your friends and school stuff your whole world.

However, the truth is, your world includes a few additional citizens. Those people you live with—you know, the ones who look vaguely like you and call you things like "sister" and "daughter"—surely you remember them.

They're your family. And although they're easy to forget about when you're daydreaming about your latest crush or your next trip to the mall, they're still an important part of your life.

According to Angelastro, making time for both friends *and* family is key. "Find time to spend with your family and friends." Angelastro said.

But what if your big brother or little sister are seriously getting to your last nerve and *clinging* to it? Everyone feels that way about siblings sometimes. But the great thing about sisters and brothers is that they know you better than anyone—since birth, usually. (Unless you had some kind of unusual grounding that involved you being imprisoned in your room for years. Which is rare.)

But because they've known you your whole life, it also means they know exactly how to push your buttons. Siblings know what to say to

Chapter 3: But Enough About History and Learning. Let's Talk About People Who Really Like Me.

make your anger level rise. Yet they also know what to say to make you crack up when you're feeling low.

If it sometimes seems like they choose the anger-inducing things to say more often, don't feel bad—you're not alone.

Sister-to-sister and brother-to-sister arguments are as old as…well, there's no historical research on that topic, but I'm pretty sure that in caveman times, at least one set of siblings argued over who last went wooly mammoth hunting and who made fire better.

Arguments are often just part of being siblings. But, believe it or not, some of that arguing is done out of love.

"Siblings can fight about anything because they feel comfortable enough to do that," Mosatche said. "Unlike friendships, in which each person can decide to be in the relationship, sibling relationships are for life."

That may sound like a prison sentence—but it's not.

As you get older, you slowly sometimes start to realize that your sibling is really one of your best friends. Your brother/sister is:

☆ Someone who knows you inside out.

☆ Someone who's always been there.

☆ Someone who knows all your embarrassing childhood secrets (unless your best friends know about that time you woke up screaming because you'd dreamt a werewolf ate part of you).

☆ Someone who will forgive you for almost anything—including sharing stories in a book about how you once dreamt a werewolf ate part of you (let's hope my sister agrees! Because that dream really freaked her out.)

☆ Someone who probably either taught you how to do something like riding a bike or drawing, or learned how to do something from you (such as how to be awesome).

☆ Someone who knows what movies, colors, foods, and other things you hate—and which ones you love.

☆ And someone who's seen your parents in pajamas. Most people in your life can't say that (unless your parents have some aversion to day clothes).

So the next time you get annoyed because your brother barged into your room—again—remember: he may be a pest, but he's also your brother. And someday—possibly not today, but eventually—you're going to be glad he is.

How to Be the Awesomest Family Member Ever

When you're living under the same roof and often feel in competition with your brothers and sisters, things can get a little heated.

Like most siblings, my sister and I had our share of arguments growing up. My parents (possibly accidentally) handled

Chapter 3: But Enough About History and Learning. Let's Talk About People Who Really Like Me.

them well: They refused to get involved whenever they could avoid it. As a result, my sister and I either talked about things until we felt better, or just chose to let it go and moved on. (Well, I once sat on my sister to end an argument, but I can't, in good faith, recommend that strategy.)

According to Harriet S. Mosatche, PhD, my parents were on to something. She recommends letting siblings resolve issues on their own—and, of course, never comparing them.

"Saying something like, 'Why can't you be an A student like Maggie is?' is the worst thing parents can do if they want siblings to get along with each other," Mosatche said.

Exactly. We all have unique talents and interests, and we're all still learning how to study, clean, balance homework and fun time, and do a bunch of other things. And, as with any learning process, that takes time. You shouldn't beat yourself up if you don't do everything perfectly the first time—and your parents shouldn't, either.

Your parents should treat you as individuals and avoid comparisons or judging. However, you may find your siblings sometimes judge your actions—and you may catch yourself judging theirs. Conflicts will undoubtedly arise, but as you both get older, they will lessen.

Growing up, my sister and I shared a bathroom, and it was the source of dozens (possibly thousands) of arguments between us. Who would get to shower first in the morning? Who didn't put the toothpaste away? Why couldn't my sister finish her hair and do her makeup in less than an hour? (I mean, other people have places to go, people to see, far more unruly hair!)

You see my point: My sister's grooming rituals took an *absolutely ridiculous* amount of time—and we found that sharing space was difficult. However, years later, after my sister and I had both gone to college and my sister had finished grad school, we decided to get an apartment together in the city.

I had several friends also moving to the same area who had offered to be my roommate—but after years of living with friends in college, I was ready to room with someone who really knew me and wouldn't worry about being too polite if I left my gloves on the floor or forgot to put my toothpaste away (even if it meant sharing a bathroom again and putting my toothpaste away).

Sure, my sister and I hadn't lived together in years. And sure, my parents expressed concern that our apartment would be littered with tufts of hair we'd pulled out of each other's heads during arguments. And sure, we had a few brief disagreements over the bathroom.

Chapter 3: But Enough About History and Learning. Let's Talk About People Who Really Like Me.

But overall, my sister was the best roommate I've ever had. Not because the others were bad, but because we were family. We liked the same TV shows and movies. We knew each other's habits, routines, weaknesses, and strengths. We were open and honest about things that upset us that we wanted to change. In fact, we successfully lived together for several years—and might still be living together if my sister hadn't gotten married and moved. (At which point I got my own apartment with my own bathroom. It was a win-win for all.)

It may sound impossible now—but someday you may view your sibling as one of your best friends. (Probably when you both learn to ward off arguments by talking about why you're upset. Or the first day that you both live in separate residences and have your own bathrooms. It helps.)

How Do You Make Your Sister Feel Super?

So you and your sister have had yet another disagreement. Things feel strained, tense and just generally bad. Why not try inviting your sister to do something fun, like a girls' day out?

Go to lunch, see a movie, get a manicure... whatever it is the two of you feel like doing (aside from feeling strained, tense and just

generally bad). Some sister bonding time can help you forget why you were even mad in the first place. (Was it that whole borrowing-your-sweater thing? Telling Mom you were late? You'll be less likely to point fingers if you can distract yourself with a new, fierce French manicure.)

Chapter 4:
HOW TO HAVE THE PERFECT SOCIAL LIFE

Chapter 4: How to Have the Perfect Social Life

School—and Its Social Scene

Technically, you're at school to learn (and, to be fair, it does involve a lot of books). However, realistically, you're getting an education in more than just math, social studies, and English. You're also learning how to interact socially with other people your age, from your area, and with similar interests. You just aren't graded on that part.

For decades, junior high and high school have offered teens a unique experience, dealing with an enclosed social scene. You work, play, and interact with your classmates on a daily basis.

Your parents (and their parents…and their parents, too) likely had a similar experiences when they were your age. But today's schools are different, according to Shilpa R. Taufique, PhD, director of the Comprehensive Adolescent Rehabilitation and Education Service (CARES) at the Child & Family Institute at St. Luke's and Roosevelt Hospitals in New York City. "Social acceptance…has become much more challenging, with increasing materialism and focus on who has what brands, gadgets, etc.," Taufique said.

No kidding. Chances are, some of your classmates place an emphasis on appearance. And it may sometimes feel like you need to wear certain looks or own certain stuff just to fit in. Keeping up with the latest fads and styles can be  lot of pressure—and it isn't always easy. Today's teens get an average allowance of $50 a week; 50 percent of teens get no allowance at all, according to a recent Ohio State University study.

Even if you're one of the lucky ones who does get an allowance, stockpiling the hottest tech gadgets and fashion trends can be a challenge. Yet pressure to focus on your appearance is just one cause of anxiety.

"Teens today face an increasing amount of stress," said Julius Licata, director of TeenCentral.net at KidsPeace, a website that offers teens and tweens help in difficult situations. (Teens post comments and questions to the anonymous site and receive responses from trained counselors and master- or doctorate-level clinicians.)

"There are issues present today that were never present in the past," Licata said. "Teens feel pressured to be successful but feel the obstacles are often overwhelming."

The hurdles you're facing may feel that way—but in reality, they are rarely too high to clear (and this is coming from someone who is 5′3″).

Chapter 4: How to Have the Perfect Social Life

So how do you find your niche without losing any sense of yourself (or becoming totally maxed out in the process)? We've got a few ideas…

Which Type Are You?
Individuals are all diverse, unique, and wonderful human beings.

Well, most of the time. The school social scene often involves a few familiar characters. And maybe people identify you as one (or more). Sure, there are some unfortunate personality choices…like The Cafeteria Fight Starter and The Girl Who Glares At You All The Time Because She Clearly Doesn't Have the Confidence or Artistic Vision to Respect Your Bold and Creative Fashion Choices.
But there are a lot of great girls in the mix, too. Do any of these descriptions sound familiar (or possibly identical to your yearbook profile)? No shame, people, no shame. There is nothing wrong with being a band geek or an athlete!

The Jock
What you know: She leads the cross country team in fall and rocks soccer and softball in spring (and plays every other sport in the months in between). She's who you'd call if you ever needed coaching; an extra intramural team member; someone to lift a car.

What you don't know: Don't dismiss the Jock as all brawn and no brains. Remember, the brain's a muscle, too. She may be strong, but she's no simple stereotype.

The Trendsetter
What you know: Her hair is always styled with an accessory you'd never even thought of using. Her outfits are so cutting edge you couldn't copy them if you tried. She knew what jeggings were before denim did.

Due to her quirky and inventive sense of style, she's got the latest looks before they hit the runways. You would call her a fashionista—*but she made up that word before you even knew it.*

What you don't know: Fashion may not be everything to this creative chica; her other interests are often more diverse than she lets on.

The Studying Star
What you know: The inside of her locker door is covered in notes; her backpack is stuffed with books—some of which she reads *for fun!*–and her calendar is filled with study-group dates. She's serious, and she's also your best bet for a tutor, should you need one at any point.

What you don't know: Despite the fact she's ultra-focused on nailing the top grade, don't assume the Studying Star is all work and no play. Once the SATs are over, she just may transition into class clown.

Chapter 4: How to Have the Perfect Social Life

The Drama Queen

What you know: But soft, what light through yonder window breaks? Why, it's the Drama Queen—and every move she makes is theatrical. She's the star of every school play and sings her heart out in the spring musical, but she's not above chipping in a performance for the annual variety show, too.

What you don't know: Just because you don't dig live theater doesn't mean you need to EXIT, STAGE LEFT. The drama queen often has friends who don't love auditioning, performing, or anything acting-related, at all.

The Green Girl

What you know: She's ecofriendly. She wears free-trade fashions and never touches food that isn't organic. She doesn't just recycle—*she got the entire school to recycle*. (Unfortunately, the schoolwide program did not include recycling the paper your last algebra test was printed on before you had to take it. But you'll ace it next time.) Your school should be proud to call this sustainable, sassy ecosoldier a student. She's keeping it real and using recyclable materials, every day. (You're welcome, Earth.)

What you don't know: She may be serious about being ecologically conscious—but that doesn't mean she's too serious to have some fun. The Green Girl frequently loves having a few laughs just as much as you do.

The Tech Genius

What you know: You just bought the latest electronic gadget. She's the one who can show you how to use it. Computer crash problems? She can fix your worst hard drive issue in 15 minutes. For the love of gigabytes, she built a computer out of pencils and sticks *for fun*! Some people have the gift of gab. She's got the gift of getting technology in a way that's both amazing and helpful. Go tech genius!

What you don't know: Just because she's most comfortable in front of a computer screen doesn't mean the Tech Genius always wants to fly solo. She craves time with her friends just like the rest of us do.

Where Do You Fit In? (And Why You Shouldn't Care.)

Once you've figured out your school's social scene—who's who, what groups are what, what activities define what groups, and

Chapter 4: How to Have the Perfect Social Life

so on—you may be wondering, *Where do I fit in?* The answer is anywhere you want to. *Snap!* (The snap is optional, but encouraged.)

In a perfect world, high school would have no cliques, no sense of social-group order, and no defined groups—just friendly, outgoing, and accepting students who want to be friends with everybody else. However, most schools do have some sort of social structure—groups that define themselves by common interests or backgrounds.

According to Julius Licata, director of teen/tween help website TeenCentral.Net at KidsPeace, that kind of unspoken social structure means that many teens have a hard time feeling like it's okay to be themselves.

"Constantly trying to fit in [is a way teens try] to avoid peer pressure, bullying, and often intimidation," Licata said.

The desire to want to be perfect is understandable. Who wouldn't want to be perfect? But perfection is a myth—which is why it's crucial not to beat yourself up about any perceived social status or other flaws you might think you have. Chances are, these alleged flaws are things that only you have noticed or worried about. The clothes you wear, the way you look, or anything else physical shouldn't define you. And the people who you go to school with shouldn't be able to define who you can or can't hang out with.

So don't let them.

How you feel is up to you. Be involved. Be enthusiastic. Be yourself. Be friendly. Be happy with the fabulous people you know, not the ones you don't.

"It's not the number of friends that matters," Taufique said. "It's the quality."

How to Be Outgoing If You're Not Really, Well, Outgoing

As you're going through the exciting (yet sometimes admittedly a little scary) journey of self-discovery that happens during your teen years (and often after), you may find your confidence is on the rise. You may, in fact, find your sense of self-confidence has swelled and built to a point where when you enter a room and people cheer to greet you, *thrilled* that one of their most self-assured, outgoing classmates has just walked in.

But if not, that's okay, too. Being confident isn't always easy. In fact, sometimes it feels really, really, *really* hard. Talking to people you don't know; going to a party by yourself; standing up in front of your history class to give a presentation.... If any of those situations sound like your worst nightmare, rest assured: you are not alone.

Chapter 4: How to Have the Perfect Social Life

Feeling more confident in social (or any other) situations takes practice and time. But with a little work, it's definitely possible.

Shilpa R. Taufique, PhD, director of the Comprehensive Adolescent Rehabilitation and Education Service (CARES) at the Child & Family Institute at St. Luke's and Roosevelt Hospitals in New York City, suggests focusing on your strengths and letting confidence come from what you inherently have to offer any relationship or situation.

Making self-confident friends can also help. "Some teens are also able to make a connection with another teen who is similar to them, but just a bit more confident and outgoing," Taufique said. "Becoming friends with this person is a great way to vicariously try out social situations that the shyer teen might not be able to do on their own."

But remember, as you branch out and build confidence, don't get too hung up on fitting in. You're a unique individual—and that's a good thing.

How to Deal with Bullying (and How Not to Be a Bully Yourself)

If you've ever been made fun of, you know that it's really not all that fun. In fact, it sucks. It really, really sucks. Even if you can laugh off a joke about yourself—or not even let it register—that kind of teasing can hurt. And unfortunately, it's not uncommon.

According to a recent study by the Josephson Institute of Ethics, 47 percent of students reported that they had been bullied, teased, or taunted. That's nearly one out of every two students!

And unfortunately, 50 percent of respondents reported bullying or teasing someone themselves.

Because technology lets you communicate with friends and others 24/7, you're exposed to more and more bullying opportunities.

"Today, a teen can be bullied all day [at school], and when they come home, turn on the computer or answer a text, it is right there. There is often no escape," Licata said.

And some people don't feel like they can fight back. Yet ignoring the problem may not make it go away. If you're being bullied, don't be afraid to ask for help. Sometimes an authority figure can help you defuse the situation.

"Clinical and research findings continue to indicate that it takes an adult to step in and set limits with a bully in order to see some change in the behaviors," Taufique said.

It may also help to realize that whoever is bullying you may have also been bullied. Although that doesn't excuse bad behavior, it may help you to see where the misplaced anger or frustration being directed at you is rooted.

"I'm finding that teens are more and more aware that bullies are former victims of bullying," Taufique said. "When working with the

Chapter 4: How to Have the Perfect Social Life

bullies directly, I find it is also most effective to set firm limits and expectations of what behavior is and is not tolerated, while also working to identify how the bully has been the recipient of similar behaviors."

According to Taufique, in 99 percent of the cases in which she directly addresses bullies, they can immediately identify the point at which they were bullied themselves. She uses the memory to help bullies empathize with their victim and break the cycle.

"There is often underlying anger and resentment that need to be dealt with as well," Taufique says. "So I find it most important to not just treat the bully as an aggressor, but also as someone who needs kindness and empathy."

Understanding a bully's inappropriate actions can help you feel better; so can choosing to only hang out with positive, supportive people whenever possible. If someone is giving you a hard time—friend, enemy, or frenemy—deal with it, and then focus on the positive things in your life: friends, family, work, school, or anything else that makes you feel happy and productive.

"Avoid people who are negative or involve themselves in negative behaviors," Licata said. "If [you] feel threatened by others through bullying, should report it—and move on."

Chapter 5:
EXCEPTIONALLY AWESOME ENTERTAINING

Chapter 5: Exceptionally Awesome Entertaining

Planning the Perfect Party

If you've ever seen an episode of MTV's *My Super Sweet 16*—and really, on a rainy day, who hasn't watched five in a row?—you know that parties have come a *loooong* way since pin the tail on the donkey.

Some girls celebrate their birthday by renting out a dance club. Or serving an elaborate, multi-tiered fondant cake. Or, you know, arriving at their party by helicopter.

Girls may be finding fresh ways to celebrate their birthday—but the practice of going all out when you turn 16 is anything but new.

"The lavish sweet sixteens started about 12 years ago—especially during MTV's show," said party planner Andrea Correale of Elegant Affairs, a New York-based full service catering and event planning company whose clients have included Russell Simmons and Mariah Carey.

Although Correale says the frenzy to plan an over-the-top sweet 16 party has died down somewhat, she still sees an interest in 16th birthday bonanzas. In addition, some of her clients also pay $1 million or more for lavish bar mitzvah and bat mitzvah bashes.

However, you don't need to spend big bucks to throw a great get-together. You just need a great idea. Start by determining what kind of party you want to throw—and how you plan to do it.

"Plan your event far in advance so you have plenty of time to work on the details," Correale said. "Don't wait until the last minute to choose what you are going to wear. Start looking ahead of time." (That will also save you from coming home to a bed covered in rejected dresses and just crawling underneath them to go to sleep because you're too exhausted to put them back in your closet. We've all been there.)

Brainstorming can help you create a truly individualized event—which is the goal. Correale suggests looking through magazines and special event books for ideas. "Rip out photos and looks that appeal to you," Correale said. "Make a list of all the things in your life that you love—from hobbies, talents, and favorite foods to your favorite season."

The party should be all about you, so do some celebration soul-searching.

"Writing these things down will help you figure out the theme or look," Correale said. "Do you picture a fun day party, 'fun in the sun', or a swanky night party? It has to scream you." (Anyone else screaming at the party, however, is not advised.)

Chapter 5: Exceptionally Awesome Entertaining

Party Types and Tips

Once you've decided what kind of party you want to plan (a big birthday bash? Small-scale celebration?), it's time to start thinking details.

Once you have your theme, you're in business. Beginning to strategize way early—like, a year ahead of time—may seem like it's too soon. However, it'll give you more options.

"You then have 12 months to find decor at bargain prices by not only searching the Internet but by asking friends and family what they may be able to contribute," Correale said. "They may have a cool prop in their garage. Who knows? Get the word out and you will be surprised what you will come up with."

Feeling overwhelmed? "Get your close friends involved to help plan the event," she said. "You can delegate and ask for help."

Cover the bases with our perfect party checklist:

Spectacular Songs

Music is key! Start by keeping a list of songs you love. If you're getting a DJ, a cheat sheet will save you from hearing "The Electric Slide" nine times. (Hopefully.)

Or opt to be your own DJ. Start stockpiling dance music and other high-energy tunes and set up a playlist on your iPod or computer. That way, when the party starts, all you have to do is push play, and you're rockin' your very own personalized mix.

Inventive Eats

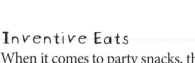

When it comes to party snacks, the best strategy is to keep it simple. You don't need to put out a ton of fancy food; you just need things that are delicious and easy to serve. It's also smart to consider the mess factor: the easier to eat, the better. "Pasta stations, burger bars, and pizza buffets are all good choices and really fun," Correale says.

One of Correale's most recent teen parties, which involved a *Charlie and the Chocolate Factory* theme, centered around creative culinary options.

In addition to the astroturf floors, oversized trees and oompa loompa breakdancers, the party décor included edible wallpaper, chocolate rivers and tabletops, napkin rings made from Dots candies and mazes of desserts cakes and candies.

"It was like you walked into the actual movie," Correale says.

How Do You Know How Much Grub to Get?
Once you've got a head count, how do you know how much food and drink to buy? A good rule of thumb is six to eight hors d'oeuvres per person and three individual bottles of soda per person, according to Correale.

A Very Cool Venue
If you decide not to have your party at home, you'll need to rent space somewhere else—which can get expensive.

Chapter 5: Exceptionally Awesome Entertaining

To save some cash, look into venues that will give you more bang for your buck. "Choose a space that already has tables and chairs so you can save on the rentals," Correale said.

Divine Décor

Once you've got a room to redo, it's time to decorate—and streamers are definitely not your only option.

Large plants can help you create a cozy ambiance. Correale suggests asking your parents to rent a helium tank and fill the ceiling of the room with color-coordinated balloons tied with ribbons, which can create an instantly festive atmosphere.

Depending on how much money is in your party fund, you may also want to pick up some extra items to add to the theme (or ask your folks to pitch in for some décor). "If you can afford it, go online and rent some specialty theme or color-coordinated designer linens," Correale says. "For a few dollars more, you could transform your room by covering you tables with unusual linens."

Another innovative idea: Decorate with something guests can munch on, such as edible centerpieces like tall glass vases filled with candy. (Flowers die. Candy lives forever.)

Lighting is also key. Use candles or colored light bulbs to set the mood—or just work your magic with the dimmer switch.

Planning an Easy Overnight Party

To jazz up a smaller-scale party, such as a sleepover, choose a festive theme like movie night.

Correale suggests renting one of those huge movie-sized screens—or even hanging a sheet in the backyard and setting up a projector. Put down blankets and provide all the treats you would get at the movie theater—real popcorn in tubs, candy, and nachos.

Perfect Party Etiquette

Parties are supposed to be fun. And it isn't 1812, so you shouldn't obsess too much about the etiquette involved. However, inviting your guests—or thanking your host—in a considerate way is never a bad thing. Being polite could, in fact, help score you an invite to the person's next party—or help boost your next bash's turnout.

Andrea Correale recommends sending an Evite to save the date. You may also want to follow up with a mailed invitation to drive the point home—something clever that announces your theme and gets everyone excited.

When you receive an invitation, always be sure to RSVP. If you've ever thrown a party, you know how helpful it is to have an accurate head count. That way you know how much food and drink to get. (You don't want to be even partially responsible for a cake shortage. Ever.)

Chapter 5: Exceptionally Awesome Entertaining

Even if you're a guest at a big bash, thanking the hostess (or host) for the great time you had is always a nice touch. No need to send snail mail if that's not your thing. An email thank-you is also appropriate—or even a shout-out on Facebook, according to Correale.

(Just don't post anything bad about a party you attended on anyone's wall—even if you have hardcore privacy settings on your account, you never know what friend of a friend may see it.)

Party Ideas That Pack a Punch

Only you can decide for yourself what the perfect party idea will be. But here are a few brilliant ideas from Correale to help you get those creative juices flowing:

13 Going on 30 Party
Featuring:
- ☆ "mocktails" in real martini glasses
- ☆ kid-friendly cuisine
- ☆ fake magazine covers with pictures of you and your friends
- ☆ And of course, Michael Jackson's "Thriller" (Dance steps optional.)

Jersey Shore Party

The guidos and guidettes on *Jersey Shore* get their "GTL" on every day; with a little preparation, you, too can do it for one magical night. (Or maybe just partake in the gym and tanning part—I may be alone in this, but I don't find doing laundry very festive.)

The menu? New Jersey boardwalk foods, obviously!
- ☆ cotton candy
- ☆ hot dogs
- ☆ French fries
- ☆ pizza

Hoping to add some activity to the event? Correale suggests setting up nets to play volleyball in the sand.

Chapter 6:
CLEVER COMMUNICATIONS

Chapter 6: Clever Communications

Why Your Parents Do Not Understand Why You Want to Text/Call So Much (and How to Avoid Getting Grounded If You Don't Have Unlimited Texting)

Your parents may roll their eyes every time they hear your phone beep when you receive a new text, but you have to understand: they grew up in a very different era.

Your parents grew up without online chatting, without cell phones, and without email. If they wanted to talk to someone, they had to pick up the phone—which was attached to the wall by a cord. And required them to use a rotary dial. (Have you ever used a rotary dial phone? It takes a full minute just to dial a seven-digit number. Who has time for that?!)

So if your mom and dad don't text—and don't get why you do—don't be too hard on them. This is a brave new world for your parents.

They might not know what BRB means, but chances are, you do. A recent study from the Pew Internet & American Life Project found that texting has become the preferred method of communicating between teens. But then, you knew that, didn't you? Here are a few other things that the study found:

☆

☆ **Most of you have cell phones.** Seventy-five percent of 12- to 17-year-olds now own them, compared to just 45 percent in 2004.

☆ **And you're using them to text.** About 88 percent of teen cell phone users text, according to the study. More than half text every day.

☆ **Sure, we all still use the phone part, too.** But two-thirds of texters say they're more likely to type a quick message to talk to their friends than to actually dial and speak with them.

Possibly because texting rarely involves sending just one message, teens are also texting a lot of messages back and forth. Half of teens say they send 50 or more texts a day—that's 1,500 a month (!). And one in three teens report sending more than 100 texts a day. (That's a lot of LOL-ing.)

The study also found that girls are more likely than boys to text. On average, we send and receive about 50 more texts a day than they do.

Chapter 6: Clever Communications

Keeping Communication Costs in Check

You may not have to deal with overage charges, because according to the Pew study, 75 percent of teens who have a cell phone have unlimited texting. If you do, awesome. Write away.

However, if you're part of the segment that has to pay per text or has a limit on how many you can send each month, you're probably aware that those FTWs add up fast.

Let's say you're just an average texter. So, you send 1,500 texts a month. If your phone company charges 10¢ for every text, so that's…I can feel the parental grounding coming now…$150 a month spent on texts. But wait—your phone company probably charges for *incoming* texts, too! So if your friends are kind people and don't ignore you when you contact them, that's $300 a month in text messaging costs! Perhaps that's why the study found that 62 percent of parents have taken their kid's phone away as punishment.

So, how can you calm mom and dad—and encourage them to allow you to keep texting? Well, you can start tracking your texts. It's tricky, but helpful. Most cell plans let you view current usage online, so you can see when you're getting close to your limit.

Asking your friends to take you off their mass "Happy Friday!" message list can also help. After all, you know it's Friday, and yes, that makes you happy, too—but you really don't need a text to know you're on the same page about the week ending.

You could also ask your parents to help you look into switching to a cell plan that offers unlimited minutes. The cost may be the same, or just slightly more—and might save some cash if you're constantly racking up overage fees. (You could also offer to contribute to the higher plan cost if you're constantly texting more than your limit. An extra $5 a month is way better than $300.)

It may help to stress to your parents that you have the phone for a reason: safety. According to the Pew study, 98 percent of parents whose children own a cell phone say they gave them phones so they could be in touch with their child at all times—a completely legitimate reason for having a phone.

Convincing your mom that you also need to use it to text friends may not be the easiest argument to win. But having the hardware is half the battle, right?

Chapter 6: Clever Communications

When Do You Call, When Do You Click?

According to the recent Pew Internet & American Life Project study, teens make or receive, on average, five cell phone calls a day.

While you're more likely to text friends than talk, the phone part is still important—especially for calling your parents. (Something about a phone call saying, "I swear I'm making it home before curfew, really, Mom" seems more convincing than a short text sent before you resume scarfing down licorice and talking about boys with your friends.)

Still, we all sometimes use our cell phone as an actual phone to call people aside from Mom and Dad. But with all the options for communication—phone, text, e-mail, chatting—how do you know which is the best way to communicate?

What's Your Communication Of Choice?
Circle your top choice:
A. Texting
B. Phone calls
C. IM/BBM/Other messaging system that involves an "m"
D. E-mail
E. Secret code
F. Carrier pigeon
G. Smoke signal
H. ESP/attempted ESP

Calmly Communicate
However you reach out, make sure you don't respond if you're

overcome with emotion. It's more difficult to convey tone in written communication like e-mails and texts, so it's easy for your message to be misinterpreted.

Never, ever text or e-mail anything when you're angry, according to Judith Belmont, M.S., a licensed psychotherapist who also works as a communication and wellness corporate trainer and speaker. "It sounds much worse when it is written," she said. "You don't have the ability to explain yourself in a face-to-face conversation; things can be misinterpreted very easily and leave a bad taste to a friendship."

Be Ready to Reply

There are no hard-and-fast rules for how you should respond to a message from a friend. However, in general, if a friend contacts you about something personal, upsetting, or really important, making contact through a phone call shows your friend that you recognize it's something she cares about—and something you care about, too.

Otherwise, consider how best to reach the person. If your friend is on her laptop all day but rarely remembers to check her phone, texting her probably isn't the best way to get in touch. The same thought process applies if she's glued to her phone but rarely logs on to Gmail. Then, chatting is most likely not your best option.

87

Chapter 6: Clever Communications

As they say (whoever that nebulous "they" are, it's true), "it's the thought that counts." So don't get too hung up on how people contact you.

Considering all the different ways to connect, chances are your friend isn't dissing you by sending you a text instead of calling—and your boyfriend isn't failing to try hard enough if he texts more than he calls. In fact, according to a 2008 AT&T survey on dating and texting, 37 percent of respondents age 18–35 reported texting at least three times a day with their significant other. Plus, 74 percent said they've flirted via text. So if your crush is sending you cute messages instead of calling you up, don't write him off just yet.

Avoiding Texting Disasters and Keeping Stuff Private

We all love taking photos.

Eighty-three percent of teen cell phone users do it, according to the Pew cell phone study. And why shouldn't we? Photos are great! It's awesome to have fun snapshots of you and your friends at parties and other events to remind you of all the incredible memories you've made in the past year. But you know what's not fun? Having a ton of people see something embarrassing or personal that you didn't want to share. You wouldn't send the entire school a photo of you in your underwear. So don't give anyone else the chance to do it.

We all know it happens: a girl sends a photo to her boyfriend. Then said boyfriend and girlfriend break up, and suddenly that very private picture message is in every in-box and cell phone in school. We cannot stress this enough. Do. Not. Go. There.

"Sexting messages might get passed around and be a huge source of embarrassment and mockery," said Judith Belmont, M.S., a licensed psychotherapist who also works as a communication and wellness corporate trainer and speaker.

Sending a nude or nearly nude photo of yourself to someone may seem like the craziest idea in the world (to be fair, it kind of is)—but clearly, some people are doing it.

Four percent of teens say they've sent a sexually suggestive nude or nearly nude image of themselves to someone via text, according to the Pew study. And those racy photos are clearly going to more than one person, because that same study found that 15 percent of teens have received a nude or nearly nude image of someone they knew via text.

Unsolicited Circulation

A study done by MTV and the Associated Press found that nearly one in five sext recipients forwarded on the images to someone else, 55 percent of those teens who sent it on did so to more than one person.

It doesn't matter if you're sending the photo to someone you trust. Things happen. The person could forward it as a mistake (we've all hit "reply all" by accident once or twice)—or for another reason. Either way, you're opening yourself up to the risk of your birthday suit being seen by a whole bunch of people.

Chapter 6: Clever Communications

Unfortunately, girls are more likely to send nude pics than boys, according to the MTV/AP study. Most often, those who had taken naked pics said they sent them to a boyfriend or crush.

The Embarrassing Aftermath
Sexting is serious—and so are the potential repercussions. According to the MTV/AP study, teens who have sexted are four times more likely to have considered suicide (four times!).

You should never, ever, EVER take a photo—or engage in any behavior—you don't want to do because someone asks you to. (Yet, in what may be today's saddest statistic, 60 percent of people who sent a nude photo said they were pressured to do so at least once. Not cool, boys, not cool.) It's important to remember that dating is not about pleasing the other person. It's about having fun (and sometimes, getting free food). If the person you like doesn't want you when you're clothed, that doesn't say much about his character. Why would you want to date someone who's pushing you to do something you don't feel comfortable doing?

Did Prince Charming ask Cinderella to send him pictures of her without her ball gown? No. Not even after it turned back into the dress she was wearing before the ball (which, let's be honest, was kind of falling apart anyway and would have been way easy to take off). What did the prince do? He walked around their town for hours just to give her shoe back. Her shoe. Now that's what I'm talkin' about.

"Nearly one in five sext recipients have forwarded the image to someone else—and 55 percent sent it to more than one person."

Sexting: Bad idea. Just don't.

Chapter 6: Clever Communications

Text Abbreviations That Should Exist

Now that we've covered the don'ts of texting, let's talk about the dos. Texting can be fun and funny. After all, we've all had times when we couldn't help but LOL—and sometimes, when we have to run an errand, we've been known to BRB.

You *could* text without using abbreviations. But why would you? They're funny—and a solid time-saver.

You know the basics. Still, there are a few that haven't found their way into common use yet that we wish people would use:

WAYTMT
Why are you texting me this?
(Seriously. I did not need to know that you are having an awesome day. Don't get me wrong, I'm glad. But next time, just tell me in homeroom.)

YMATCAYIT
Your mom's about to call, and you're in trouble.
(Okay, so it's not fair to expect your friends to be able to know that ahead of time when you don't. But wouldn't it be awesome if they could send you a warning text?)

IHM
I hate Mondays.
(We all do. But unless you're Garfield, add this quickie onto the end of a text instead of wasting an entire message to tell people you're anti-first-day-of-the-week.)

ILC
I like cupcakes.
This shows the text recipient that you're brilliant because cupcakes are delicious.

LTMTJOWSWDUHYMTA
Let's text more than just one word so we don't use half your monthly text allowance.
(I only get 100 texts a month. So I cringe every time someone texts me "Good morning." That's only 99 more, people!)

[INSERT NAME HERE] LSCT
[BOY NAME OF YOUR CHOICE] looked super cute today. (Just keep this one in the ready-to-copy/paste file, people.)

TMIGAFS
The mall is giving away free shoes!
(A girl can dream…)

ITYBTPNTMITRLOHP
I'm texting you because the person next to me is talking really loudly on her phone.
(You get points for being considerate—especially if you're on the bus. There's nothing like learning that the person next to you just had the worst lunch ever. Did her friend need to know that? Probably not. Did you? Unless you prepared it for or served it to her, then no.)

IJSYAL
I just sent you a letter.
(Because it's nice to get real mail sometimes.)

Chapter 6: Clever Communications

TGTLY
That guy totally likes you.
(Because, um, stop being insecure, he fully does.)

Because You Can't Text All the Time

If you've ever wondered how people communicated in high school before texting was an option, you may be surprised to find out it involved writing notes—on paper.

Sure, it's not very green. But writing (and passing) notes is quickly becoming a lost art form—which is a shame. Not that I advise writing secret messages to your friends instead of paying attention in class, mind you. Learning is important; don't get me wrong. But if you're going to exchange thoughts somehow during the day…it doesn't always have to be via phone. (And, should you somehow find yourself having an absolute need to talk to someone during class, and if your school's banned cell phone usage during the day, chances are, you're less likely to get busted slipping a small note to someone than you are whipping out your phone to text a message. I'm just sayin'.)

Not skilled in the art of note passing? No worries. We've got some tips and tricks to help you learn.

Classic Note-Folding Shapes

When I was in high school (which was a few years ago—but not too long ago to remember just how frantic it could feel when you had news to share and were stuck in study hall), note-folding was practically an artistic talent.

Sure, there might have been times when I just folded a piece of notebook paper in half and handed it to somebody. But in most cases, folding your note into a variety of shapes—like an arrow, or a heart, or a triangle—took as long, if not longer, than writing the actual note.

Of course, you can just fold your note a few times and call it a day. But if you're into origami, or have friends who will appreciate the effort, there's an endless amount of shapes you can craft your note into. Such as:

The Arrow
It's as if your note says "I'm pointing this way to HUGE GOSSIP! Which is inside. So unfold me."

Directions:
- ☆ Fold the paper in half the long way.
- ☆ On each end of the rectangle, fold each corner in to make a triangle.
- ☆ Pinch together at the crease (the top of the paper will look like the hood to a cape). At the same time, fold down the top of the other side of the paper to make an arrowhead. Press down to flatten.
- ☆ Do the exact same thing to the other end to create a second arrowhead.
- ☆ This is the tricky part: Fold in each side of the long center rectangle to overlap and make a thinner rectangle.
- ☆ Fold the entire thing in half at the middle and tuck the bottom arrowhead into the top arrowhead to secure.

Chapter 6: Clever Communications

ARROW

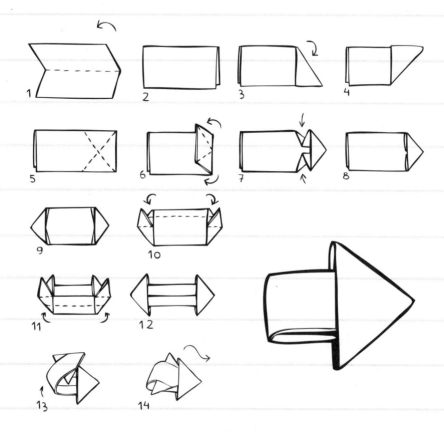

The Heart

Forget about those kidney- and liver-shaped notes you've been sending. When it comes to messages shaped like body parts, the heart is where it's at.

Directions:

☆ With the paper in front of you vertically, fold the right and left corners in and squeeze together in the center where the creases you just made meet. The resulting paper should look like an arrow with a big top and short bottom.

Chapter 6: Clever Communications

- ☆ Fold the right and left corners of the arrow top up to create a kite-shaped fold.

- ☆ Fold the left side in to line up with the side of the kite-shaped part. Do the same thing on the right.

- ☆ Fold the bottom half up so it touches the bottom of the kite-shaped part.

- ☆ Flip the note over and fold the pointed arrow point down.

- ☆ Take the lower left corner and fold it up to touch the bottom point of the part you just folded down (toward the center). Do the same thing on the other side.

- ☆ That folded part on the right you made in the last step? Pull it and tuck it into the top flap (the one you made in step 5). Do the same thing with the folded part on the left side – only fold it and tuck it across the entire into the same flap.

- ☆ Then fold the upper left and right points of the triangle down toward the bottom of the heart, and tuck them into the piece you pulled across the entire heart at the end of step 7.

- ☆ Awww. You made a heart.

The Classic Mailbox

Directions:
- ☆ Fold upper right corner downward so that the paper is flush on the left side. Press to crease.

- ☆ Grabbing bottom right corner, fold paper over so that edge is flush with the left edge.

★ Hold paper at bottom left edge of the diagonal fold. Tuck everything underneath below.

★ Now, fold top over the segment underneath.

★ Keep rolling until you're left with one little tab—your mailbox flag—to tuck into the diagonal.

★ Mail you mailbox. This is all so meta!

Passing Note

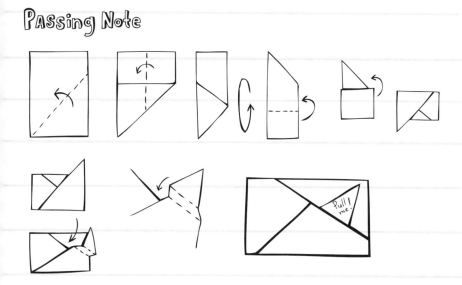

Chapter 7:
BEING CONFIDENT

Chapter 7: Being Confident

Are You?

Confidence can be a tricky thing to master. Not impossible, mind you—just challenging. So if you don't currently consider yourself bold, brazen, and generally unstoppable, it's okay. You may in time.

Just *how much* time that transition will take depends on a number of factors. How outgoing are you? And how outgoing do you want to be? (By the way, there's absolutely nothing wrong with being a little shy sometimes. Even the most confident people are in certain situations.)

Are you comfortable meeting new people? Or does the very thought of it make you cringe? Are you the kind of girl who can't remember ever feeling uncomfortable in a crowd? Or are you more likely to take a position in the corner and watch from the sidelines?

There's no right or wrong answer to those questions. And if you're feeling a little on the shy side, rest assured, that's a totally normal place to be.

"Teen girls—in any generation—notoriously have general self-esteem and self-confidence issues [because it is] time of strong

you are

hormonal changes and physical and emotional transition," communication and wellness corporate trainer and speaker Judith Belmont, M.S. said.

As you figure out who you are, what you like, what you want, and what you don't, you'll begin to find your voice and become more self-confident.

So don't beat yourself up for not being the life of the party at every single event—learning when you want to lay low and when you want to shout out loud is all part of the process.

Confidence: Fake It to Make It

You may not be naturally confident. But in reality, the only person who knows that is you. And, as my friend Michelle always says, fake it until you are. (I think she was actually talking about making people at work believe that you're not tired—but the same principle applies.)

Chapter 7: Being Confident

"Working at developing yourself always results in higher self-confidence," Belmont said.

The reason? The more experiences you have, the more things you learn—and the more you grow personally. "You are focusing on developing yourself and your character," Belmont said. "And if you work hard to pursue things that interest you, your self-concept improves as you are 'proactive' rather than 'reactive.'"

Centering your sense of confidence on how you feel about yourself—and not how you think others perceive you—is the shortest route to being a confident person.

Learning new things can help give your sense of self-assurance a big boost.

But most important of all, it should be about you. Don't compare yourself to someone else, or to an ideal. Accept your strengths along with your shortcomings. And work hard to be the best you that you can be.

"The less you look to others for approval, the more you focus on liking yourself, and [you let your] self-esteem grow," Belmont said. "Never give anyone too much power over your self-esteem. Like yourself and likely others will, too!"

Secrets of Super-Confident People

The secret to being truly confident is to know that even the most self-assured person sometimes feels insecure. It's what makes us human (and not conceited).

High school and junior high can be particularly hard on your self-esteem. You're often starting at a new school, which means having to start over socially. You're meeting a ton of new people

Chapter 7: Being Confident

and may be faced with some exciting (yet sometimes terrifying) opportunities like joining new activities, dating and more.

It's inevitable that difficulties will arise when adapting to a new environment. Often, people look to what others are doing as a way to fit in and cope.

"In wanting to be liked and accepted, often teen girls compare themselves too much to superstar teens, beautiful teen models, the popular girls at school—and find themselves often falling short on many levels," Belmont said.

Don't do it. People are unique, interesting individuals for a reason—so don't let your insecurities convince you otherwise.

The last thing you want is for other people's opinions of you to become the basis for your self-esteem. You wouldn't hand over your room or your bike or your favorite dress to someone, would you? So why hand over your ego?

One potential solution: Join clubs, sports, or other organizations. It's an easy way to join a network and contribute your talents. You'll also enjoy the company of other people who share similar interests.

And remember, overwhelming, incredible self-esteem doesn't happen overnight—but it can be achieved.

As Belmont says, although confidence is not something we are necessarily born with, certain personality types are more optimistic and tend to be more accepting and less self-critical. The rest of us have to work at it.

A Quick Guide To Instantly Upping Your "Wow" Factor

If you're looking for a confidence quick-fix, try the following tips:

- ☆ Treat yourself to something nice. Buy a new sweater. Splurge on some shoes. Or just partake in a super-delicious, topping-laden ice cream treat. The point is to do something to make yourself happy—because the happier you feel, the happier you come across to people. (Everybody wins!)

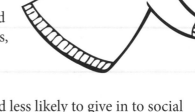

- ☆ Share any insecurities with people you trust. Sometimes just unloading a problem makes you feel better. Saying something out loud can make it feel less scary, serious, or stressful.

- ☆ Stay involved. "Extracurricular activities can keep [you] busy and less likely to give in to social pressures during idle time," Belmont says.

- ☆ Consider counseling. If you feel overwhelmed, consider talking to someone. Your school counselor is there for more than just

Chapter 7: Being Confident

giving out college applications. "If you find shyness gets in the way of developing friendships, a therapist is invaluable to help you practice social skills and identify negative self-talk that gets in the way of your confidence," Belmont said.

☆ Work to slowly overcome shyness by making new friends. Look for people who share similar interests with you—that's a great place to start. And if the thought of meeting new people stresses you out, remember that you don't have to be instant best friends. Just focus on adding some new, fun experiences to your social life.

☆ Hold your ground and don't do things that make you feel uncomfortable. Trying new things and being more outgoing doesn't mean you have to do anything you don't want to do— like drink at a party, or lie to your parents, or change what you believe in.

Chapter 8:
LIVING A HEALTHY LIFE

Chapter 8: Living a Healthy Life

How Healthy Are You?

Being healthy doesn't just involve taking a daily vitamin and eating the occasional salad. Or does it? Take the quiz, below, and find out just your nutritional nirvana level.

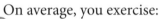

You're *starving*. For a snack, you grab:
a. An apple.
b. A low-fat yogurt, which you mix with some candy.
c. A giant chocolate chip cookie.

On average, you exercise:
a. An hour a day.
b. A couple of times a week.
c. What's this "exercise" thing you're talking about?

You tend to sleep:
a. A solid 8 to 10 hours a night, always.
b. 7 hours a night.
c. Hardly ever. Your bed misses you.

Which are you fairly sure is the healthiest thing on this list?
a. 1/3 cup of cashews or iceberg lettuce with ¼ c. ranch dressing.
b. One 12-ounce diet soda.
c. Six small candy bars.

How stressed would you say you are most days?
a. Cool as a cucumber.
b. Depends on the day, but sometimes, a total stressball.
c. WHY ARE YOU ASKING ME QUESTIONS WHEN I HAVE SO MANY THINGS TO GET DONE?!

Which of the following do you get the most of each day, eating-wise?
a. Fruits and vegetables.
b. Carbs and some fats.
c. Sugars and fats.

In general, for meals, which of the following do you eat the most?
a. Stuff I cooked or that my parents cooked, using fresh produce and other ingredients.
b. A mixture of home-cooked meals, frozen dinners, and take-out.
c. Primarily fast food. If it doesn't come in a container, it doesn't go into my mouth.

Answers

If you answered mostly As: You are a health master. No, seriously. You're eating really well, exercising regularly (even sometimes meeting the recommended daily amount of physical activity), and sleeping a ton. All of those factors help you avoid stress. So rock on with your bad self! You may have one or two health habits you could improve upon, but you're headed in the right dietary and health direction.

If you answered mostly Bs: Good news: You're partway there! You have some super-healthy habits, which is great, and some things you could work on, too. But life is about balance. With a few tweaks, you'll be able to easily kick your health status up a notch or two!

If you answered mostly Cs: Maybe it's just been a rough few weeks for you. Or maybe you've picked up some not-so-healthy habits from friends or family. No worries, though—you may not be a

Chapter 8: Living a Healthy Life

good-health goddess just yet, but with a few changes, you can feel fantastic!

Why You Can't Put Off Living Healthfully

Wait a second, you're thinking. I'm young. I have plenty of time to correct any poor health habits I might have. Right?

It's easy to live in the present—especially when that present includes pizza and a jumbo-sized Coke. But being aware of what you're putting into your body is important.

Life can be hectic, says Carolyn Dean, MD, ND, author of *The Future Health Now Encyclopedia* and *The Complete Natural Guide to Women's Health*. "[Teens deal] with four bodies: the chemical/physical body, digital/Internet body, TV body, and astral body. They are trying to feed all their bodies with information/food and…[the] physical body…suffers the most abuse."

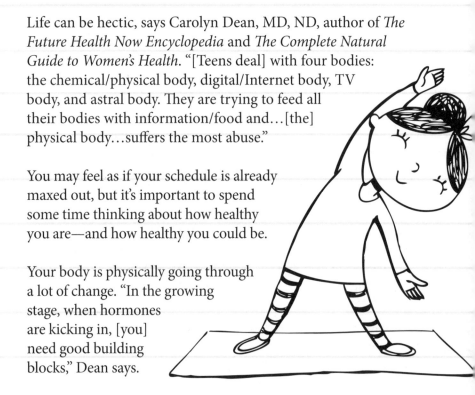

You may feel as if your schedule is already maxed out, but it's important to spend some time thinking about how healthy you are—and how healthy you could be.

Your body is physically going through a lot of change. "In the growing stage, when hormones are kicking in, [you] need good building blocks," Dean says.

You may feel okay today, but that doesn't mean you couldn't potentially improve your nutrition, exercise and other aspects of your health regimen. (Who couldn't stand to adopt a few more healthy behaviors?) Read on for some suggestions…

Small Ways to Make Big Changes in Your Health

If all this talk about the importance of exercise and eating right is starting to panic you, take a deep breath. The last thing your body needs is additional stress!

Here are some foolproof tips to help you add some healthy habits to your life:

Get plenty of sleep. Whether you're trying to lose or just maintain a healthy weight, sleep is crucial, according to Sarah Krieger, MPH, RD, LD/N. Always make time for *at least* seven hours of sleep each night. Eight to ten is even better.

Plan a balanced schedule. You only have so many hours in the day; use them wisely. Plan your day ahead of time to help avoid stress and predetermine your priorities.

And remember, there may be nine interesting things you want to join, but be careful not to overload your (already precious) free time.

"For girls who want to be involved in every sport or club, for example, the teen years are a time to practice choosing just one or two extracurricular activities at a time," Harriet S. Mosatche, PhD, said. "That kind of practice in decision-making will serve girls well

Chapter 8: Living a Healthy Life

as they face a lifetime of such hard choices."

Make healthy eating part of your daily routine. "Cut back on sugar and stop diet products," said Carolyn Dean, MD, ND. She suggests noshing on nuts, seaweed, and seeds—all of which are high in magnesium—and fish such as wild salmon, which is high in omega-3 fatty acids.

Learning more about nutrition can also help you make smarter cuisine choices. Check out www.nutrition.gov for the truth about what you're *really* eating, smart tips on how to navigate the school cafeteria menu, and more.

Plan ahead to avoid overeating. We've all been there. You're in a rush, you're starved, and to calm your growling stomach, you cram down a huge meal…and when it all settles, you're completely stuffed. Way stuffed. Feeling-awful stuffed.

"The bottom line is [people] may be going too long in between meals and overeat high-sugar/high-fat foods when they do eat," Krieger said.

Try out a snack-based system or substitute healthier alternatives to your current snacks to help you adopt new, healthier habits. One potential solution Krieger suggests is to keep nutritious foods in your purse or backpack for school to prevent major hunger. A good rule of thumb: don't go more than three or four hours between meals. (And no, gum doesn't count.)

When you're reaching for a snack, think about nuts, apples, oranges, or granola. Foods like yogurt, string cheese, or fruit smoothies are great choices to replenish nutrients in your system at that crucial three-hour mark.

Try making one change at a time. And if you have an off day, don't give up. "Take a good look at your eating habits," Krieger said. "If you drink a lot of soda (more than 12 oz. a day), try drinking water or unsweetened green tea instead. If the first meal of the day is eaten at 2:00 PM, aim for a cheese stick and apple before school starts."

And remember to focus on your overall health habits. If you have an off-day, don't give up. Healthy living is a process.

Okay, So What Nutrients Do I Absolutely, Positively Have to Get?

☆ **Calcium:** "Bones are growing at a rapid rate at [your] stage. Choose fat-free versions of chocolate milk, yogurt, and cheese and replace soda for chocolate milk for a sweet, nutrient-rich drink," Krieger said.

Chapter 8: Living a Healthy Life

- ☆ **Iron:** Your impending (or developing) growth spurt and muscular needs mean your body has a greater demand for iron-rich foods, according to Krieger. "Aim for iron-fortified cereals, lean beef, chicken, and pork, as well as a variety of veggies—beans and spinach, for example," she said.

- ☆ **Omega-3 fatty acids:** "Heart disease can develop at an early age," Krieger said. "Start now to include marine or plant fats most days of the week instead of saturated fats."

All About Exercise

When the U.S. Department of Health and Human Services and the CDC conducted its recent National Youth Risk Behavior Survey (YRBS)—which monitors six categories of health-risk behaviors among young adults—23 percent of respondents reported that they did not participate in 60 minutes or more of physical activity in the week before the survey was taken.

That's too bad—because the federal government's 2008 Physical Activity Guidelines for Americans suggest getting 60 minutes a day of exercise (mostly aerobic, with muscle strengthening and bone strengthening exercises mixed in during the week for good measure).

Don't beat yourself up too much if you're not making your goal. First of all, I was basically inert until about age 18, so I'm not one to judge. And secondly, only 35 percent of adults 18 and over engage in regular leisure-time physical activity, according to the Center for Disease Control's 2009 Summary Health Statistics for U.S. Adults: National Health Interview Survey. (And don't let the term "leisure-time" fool you: That doesn't include sleep. Unfortunately.)

An hour of exercise a day may seem like a lot, but before you panic, remember: gym class counts. Aiming to get 60 minutes of exercise each day will at least ensure you're getting regular physical activity, which can help you reduce your stress level, give you more energy, and help you sleep better at night. If you get less, give yourself an "A" for effort—and keep trying. Making the commitment to be fit is half the battle.

Exercising does many wonderful things: including helping you avoid all of the issues regularly associated with obesity, including high blood pressure, insulin resistance, diagnosed diabetes, sleep apnea, and joint problems.

Krieger suggests making your daily exercise activity fun so it's something you will enjoy and look forward to doing—like playing Wii, shooting hoops, or just taking a walk around the neighborhood while zoning out to whatever's on your iPod (or on your mind).

"If exercise becomes a chore and not something that is fun and makes you tired, then cut back a bit," Krieger said. "If you hate all fitness, keep trying until you find something that is fun."

Chapter 8: Living a Healthy Life

Ways To Re-Energize Your Exercise Routine

☆ Make a new music mix of dance songs.

☆ Splurge on new workout shoes or a fun new workout outfit.

☆ Set a time goal for yourself to run for 30 minutes, swim for 20, etc.

☆ Try a totally new type of exercise via a class: pilates, yoga or something entirely different.

Chapter 9:
BEAUTYRAMA

Chapter 9: Beautyrama

Your Hair: A Lifelong Struggle

It's an unspoken rule of life that at some point you'll decide that you want the complete opposite type of hair than you have naturally. If you've got curly hair, you probably are dying for a straight 'do. And if you have stick-straight hair, there's a high probability that you might someday crave curls. (I don't think I gave much thought before my junior year of high school to what college I wanted to attend, but I always had a plan for what my hair would look like in the next six months.)

Thanks to technology and the wide array of styling products on the market today, you can radically change your hair to pretty much any style you want. (Or, if all else fails, get a really high-quality wig.) However, there are a few things to consider before you start feathering, adding highlights, or flat ironing.

You don't necessarily need to shampoo your hair daily. I know that may sound weird, but you don't want to strip your hair of all the nifty natural oils you're producing.

Mario Tricoci—who owns 19 Mario Tricoci salons in Chicago and Kansas, launched the Tricoci University of Beauty Culture beauty school in 2004, and has been featured in publications like *Vogue*,

Elle, and *Glamour*—says you should really only wash your hair every second or third day.

Washing your hair too frequently may actually make it feel greasier. "Sometimes teens with oily skin and hair wash, wash, and wash more thinking that will help get rid of the oils when in fact, it causes the scalp to go into protection mode and actually produce more oil," said Amy Quackenbush, a Seattle-based stylist with over 12 years' experience. "Our scalp wants to naturally feel hydrated, and it knows how to do that on its own. So take the oil away constantly, and it works harder to produce more." In short: give the scalp what it wants. Give the scalp what it wants!!!

Get frequent trims. It's clear when you need a cut if you have a short 'do. However, longer hair also requires frequent trims, even if you're desperate for it to be longer. "Obviously, if you are wearing your hair super-short like Emma Watson or Michelle Williams, you will need more frequent trips to the salon to maintain that style," Quackenbush said. "With longer hair, the ends have been exposed to way more elements—blow drying, flat ironing, wind, sun, etc.—so those ends need regular trimming, as well."

"People that especially want to have long hair must have it cut often," Tricoci said. "I don't mean cut *off*—[but] trim the ends, shape the hair,

Chapter 9: Beautyrama

and condition the hair properly. It allows hair to grow." He suggests getting a half-inch snipped off every two months.

And you don't have to book a salon appointment to do it if you're trying to save cash. "If your mother cuts your hair, that's fine, too," Tricoci said.

Deep condition occasionally. Use a daily conditioner each time you wash your hair. And if you're doing a lot of heat styling such as frequent blow drying or flat ironing (and who isn't doing frequent blow drying and flat ironing; I've been using flat irons since they were so new that they basically involved plugging a crocodile into the wall and using it's teeth to comb your hair), it can't hurt to do a home deep-conditioning treatment every once in a while.

"When you shampoo your hair every day and you have to dry it and flat iron, you're really stripping your hair of its natural sheen and oil," Tricoci said. "You have to then use an artificial component to get shine back in your hair."

He suggests using a deep conditioning treatment and either using a blow dryer to add some heat or wrapping your hair in a plastic bag to provide some natural heat. That way, the conditioning fully penetrates the core of your hair.

If you must flat iron, be fast. You wouldn't leave an iron sitting on a shirt; it would burn the fabric. So don't let that flat iron linger on your luscious locks.

"The moment you put the flat iron to your hair, [be sure to] move it at the same time," Tricoci said. (The same thing goes for curling irons, too.)

Coating your hair first with a styling lotion product that contains silicone (but one that doesn't contain much alcohol, which heats up quickly) can also help protect hair.

Give your hair some space. "Instead of applying [direct] heat to the hair, dry your hair like you're in the wind, [holding the dryer] at least six inches away from hair to start off with," Tricoci said. "And when you need to style hair, bring it a bit closer."

If you're gonna do color, don't overdo it. According to Tricoci, it's totally fine to highlight your hair with some natural shades. However, if you're hoping to drastically alter your hair color, you'll have to first have to bleach it to remove all the color—then you can add the new color back in. Not only is it a complicated process, it's one that is hard on your hair. And you do not want the outcome to be Straw City, population: You.

"Coloring hair at 12-13 years of age, [I wouldn't advise you] make a radical change and bleach your hair and make it pink because you have to take the color out and redeposit color," Tricoci said. "But you can do some highlights in the sense of creating variation of shade."

Chapter 9: Beautyrama

Consider doing something a little less drastic such as adding a few strands of lighter red and another slightly lighter tone to reddish-brown hair—which will also look more natural as it grows out.

Make sure your appointment includes a consultation. You need to communicate with your stylist before the cut happens to let the stylist know what you want—and bringing photos of looks you like is a great idea. (I always do. You want your new haircut to make you feel unmistakeable—not misunderstood.)

"Bringing pictures is always a huge help," Quackenbush said. "By bringing in examples of what you like, and even *don't* like, you and your stylist can communicate and visually look at examples together."

Make sure to ask questions if anything is unclear. And if the new 'do looks more like a don't (or even worse, an *oh no she dihn't*), speak up.

"Don't be afraid to communicate with your stylist about how you feel about your cut," Quackenbush said. "I know it can be intimidating, and if you're nervous in person, don't hesitate to call when you get home and ask to speak to the manager or owner."

Many times, a cut can be fixed. The haircut may just be styled differently than you expected—might just need a few snips to alter the way it falls.

Short on funds? Consider a beauty school. "Beauty schools are great opportunities," Tricoci said. "You're dealing with students who want to be professional and a teacher who is obligated to do the right thing, so there is the opportunity to get your hair cut and done at a fraction of the price and get the professional point of view."

When styling, practice makes perfect. "Be a bit patient," Tricoci said. If your first attempt at flat ironing or silky waves is a total bust, keep trying until you nail the look—and make sure you're taking care of your hair.

"If it doesn't work the first time, go back and understand what the rules are to do hair," he says. "Don't overdry it, condition it often and get a haircut. A lot of times that's the answer why hair won't behave for you." (It's true: grounding hair rarely works.)

> ### Tools of the Trade
> Tricoci suggests investing in the following hairstyling helpers to tame your mane:
>
> **A good brush:** Brushing is key because it helps spread the natural oil from your scalp throughout your hair for shine. Use a brush that has both nylon and natural boar bristles, not one made of metal or other artificial bristles. It might run you a little bit extra, but it'll last for years.

Chapter 9: Beautyrama

> **Tools of the Trade – Continued**
>
> **Fabric-friendly elastics:** If you're a ponytail addict, don't ever use rubber bands. Instead, look for hair elastics that are cloth-covered. That way, you'll reduce the wear-and-tear on your hair. It's bad enough that the everyday elements create split ends. You don't want split *middles*, too, do you?
>
> **Use flat hair clips.** If you separate your hair using clips to dry it in sections (which can help you dry it evenly), Tricoci prefers using flat clips instead of ones with tiny teeth. Those teeth may hold better in your hair, but make it harder to smooth hair when drying it.

Makeup: What You Need to Know

Even if you clocked some significant time slathering blue eye shadow on your childhood Barbie dolls beauty styling head (or perhaps yourself), you may still wonder if there are some magical tips and tricks that can help you master makeup usage.

Good news: There are! When it comes to makeup, you can always learn more ways to put it on.

According to New York–based makeup artist Belinda Moss, who has beautified celebs such as Scarlett Johansson, Eva Longoria, Gisele Bündchen, and Beyoncé, the tween years are a great time to start getting creative with cosmetics. She suggests starting out subtly with sparkly lip glosses in pink and neutral colors.

"I recommend that girls play 'makeup artist' with their friends and family and try out different colors," Moss said. "They'll receive feedback from the people close to them about what looks good or bad."

Speaking of what looks bad—consider going easy on your eye makeup. Moss says one of the most common mishaps she sees is too much eyeliner, what she calls "a smoky eye gone wrong." You want your eye makeup to look smoky—not like you've given yourself two black eyes.

"It might work on [your] favorite rock star performing on stage, but in everyday [use], it looks ridiculous," she said.

Face Forget-Its

Belinda Moss suggests having fun and trying out new types of makeup to see what works best. And you absolutely should.

However, she also offers the following, "hmmm, maybe-you-should-just-skip-it" make-up tips. You probably never want to:

☆ Use an eyeliner for a lip liner.

☆ Share your mascara. (It could spread germs that could potentially lead to eye infections.)

☆ Use liquid eyeliner unless you know how. (Practice first! It can be an intense look.)

Chapter 9: Beautyrama

Face Forget-Its – continued
- ☆ Wear bright red matte lipstick. (Well, maybe not just yet ...)
- ☆ Overpluck your eyebrows.
- ☆ Use makeup to look 30 when you're 13. You've got plenty of time—and lipstick shades to try—before you get there.

Amazing Hair and Makeup Tips

If you've never used eyeliner, blush, lip liner, or any other kind of makeup before, be aware that practice makes perfect. Which is great, because practice can also be fun. If you dig art, it's kind of like painting—only the canvas is your face. (Don't use actual paint, though. That would be a bad idea.)

If your friends, mom, or other girls you know aren't huge beauty junkies—and you've saved enough to splurge on a new lip gloss or eye shadow—department store beauty departments are a great resources.

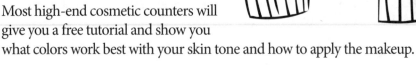

Most high-end cosmetic counters will give you a free tutorial and show you what colors work best with your skin tone and how to apply the makeup.

Many even allow you to call ahead of time for an appointment. (You don't technically have to buy anything, but I always feel weird getting glammed up and not shelling out for at least one item.)

However, you don't need to spend a ton to learn how to use makeup or new ways to accent your best features. Consider these additional beautification tips:

Wash frequently for clear skin
"Teens tend to have oily skin—they need to keep the skin clean, cleanse it," says Mario Tricoci, owner of the Mario Tricoci salons, and founder of the Tricoci University of Beauty Culture.

Moss advises washing your face daily and using a moisturizer with sunscreen to help keep your skin fresh. And don't go overboard with the exfoliation. Chances are, you really don't need it.

"The key thing is to, instead of covering it up with makeup, get beautiful skin," Tricoci says.

Eat right for a killer complexion. What you munch on also contributes to your complexion. We may all love junk food, but try to splurge on it in moderation. So the next time you reach for that soda, at least consider grabbing a bottle of water instead.

The Future Health Now Encyclopedia and *The Complete Natural Guide to Women's Health* author Carolyn Dean recommends cutting out "refined foods and sugar and eating more greens and whole grains" to cure dull hair and skin.

Consider getting a facial. If you're not sure you want to head to the dermatologist just yet, considering booking a facial to get a skin boost—and some tips.

Chapter 9: Beautyrama

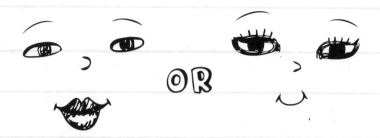

Utilize acne aids. Dean suggests using a clay face pack to calm a bad breakout. Sure, you'll look a little freaky briefly. But it's worth it. (Who knew mimes knew so much about facial care?)

Get ready to radiate. "Shimmer in the center of the eyelid and the bow of the upper lid is so pretty," Moss said. "The whole idea is to use that glow from within—and at [your] age, you can't help but glow."

Looking for a trendy tip? Try a new tint. "A hot look right now for teens is colored mascaras," Moss said. "Even if you do just the tips in a pretty blue or burgundy, [your] eyes will pop when the light hits them."

Never go to bed with makeup on. This benefits not only you, but also your sheets. No matter how tired you are, get out your washcloth and facial cleanser and scrub that face every night. It's the surest way to avoid breakouts, bad skin—and a mascara-smeared pillow.

And remember, less is more. Putting on a ton of makeup doesn't always mean you look more glam. Sometimes just using neutral shades that are applied lightly can have a big impact. "A natural look goes a long way, and a classic beauty is always 'in,'" Moss said.

And, Of Course, Inner Beauty Is the Most Important Thing

Makeup, inventive hairdos, and creative fashion looks can be really fun to try on. However, while sparkly hot pink lip gloss can be a good time, don't forget that there's something even more important that will make your skin look perfect and hair seem even shinier: our old friend inner beauty. And you don't need a single eye shadow shade to bring that out.

Unfortunately, many girls spend a significant amount of time (really, any amount of time is too much) worrying about how they look—and how other people look.

But that is a bad idea! A really, really, really, super-huge, ginormous, unbelievably *bad idea*!

Sure, you can always find someone who is taller, or who you think is thinner, or someone who has smaller feet than you. But you're most likely being way overcritical about how you look—and in time, as you get older and see things a little bit differently, believe me, you won't even remember why you focused on certain perceived "flaws."

Chapter 9: Beautyrama

I, for example, was obsessed with my nose in high school. I was convinced that's what everyone stared at when they first met me. I agonized over photos of it, convinced that some revealed its true mammoth size. I wouldn't even walk down the cereal aisle at the grocery store for fear someone would mistake me for Toucan Sam. I begged for surgery to have my nose reduced. My parents never agreed to let me have one.

Years later, I finally did have surgery—sinus surgery, to correct a ridiculously deviated septum that had been causing me breathing problems since birth and to enlarge my sinus openings. And here's the secret about surgery, of any kind: it hurts—a lot. So now, I'm just glad that I've healed and that my nose works like it's supposed to. (I could care less if I woke up tomorrow and looked an anteater. Really).

The truth is, the body part you're focusing on and worrying about is probably something other people haven't even noticed. Seriously. Even if you're convinced it is the *first* thing people see when you walk into a room. Even if you're sure it's the one thing that's keeping you from being a supermodel. Trust me, it isn't.

One of my previous jobs involved helping to hire models for photo shoots. You may not realize it, but models have bad hair days, unexpected breakouts, and dorky glasses—all the same things we deal with.

Models aren't perfect; they have just as many insecurities as you do. Maybe more, because people are staring at their face and body every day when they go to work—which is enough to make anyone a little self-conscious. (However, they get to travel a lot and get free clothes sometimes, so it kind of balances things out.)

Girls often have a tendency to zone in on certain things when it comes to ourselves—but people, in general, take in the big picture. Think about it: When you meet someone, do you assess whether they seem nice, put together, funny, cool—or do you immediately start thinking about how the person appears to have uneven elbows, and how that's absolutely ruining her chance of ever being good-looking?

Exactly. You're more concerned with hearing how your friend knows her and finding out where she got those great pants, so you can pick up a pair, too, because they'd go perfectly with that shirt you just bought at 60 percent off and those shoes you found last week in the back of your closet that you thought you'd left at…You get the picture.

Chapter 10:
STUDY HABITS OF THE RICH AND FAMOUS (OR, AT LEAST ACADEMICALLY SUCCESSFUL)

Chapter 10: Study Habits of the Rich and Famous (or at Least Academically Successful)

Five Things You May Be Doing When Studying That Aren't Helping

If you're doing any of the following while studying, you probably aren't giving yourself the best educational experience:

1. Watching TV

Curse you, fascinating television programming! TV is always tempting. In fact, watching TV is the most popular leisure activity in the U.S., according to the U.S. Bureau of Labor Statistic's 2009 American Time Use Survey. Americans ages 15 and over watched an average of 2.8 hours of television a day, half of their allotted amount of daily leisure time.

However, watching while you're studying may distract you from what you're trying to memorize, read, or write. (After all, isn't the whole point of watching a show to watch it? You can't do that and keep your eyes on that homework. Unless your homework assignment is to watch TV. But chances are, it's not.)

2. Talking on the phone

According to Bobbi DePorter, co-founder of the learning and life skills summer program SuperCamp, president of Quantum Learning Network, and author of more than a dozen books including *The Seven Biggest Teen Problems and How to Turn Them Into Strengths*, study breaks are a good idea.

"Studies show that you remember best what you learned just before and just after a break—so the more breaks, the more you learn," she said.

However, if you find that you're breaking every few seconds because your phone is ringing off the hook,
you're not going to get anything done—so try and set aside a specific time to stop and do a voicemail check, such as 30 minutes into studying.

3. Taking frequent text or e-mail breaks
Time consultant Christine Louise Hohlbaum, author of *The Power of Slow: 101 Ways to Save Time in Our 24/7 World*, says it's important to remove potential distractions.

"We all know how enticing Facebook can be," Hohlbaum said. "But to tune into your work you've got to tune out the online world. So flip the switch."

4. Listening to music
While I generally think music makes everything better (parties, driving, awkward situations, *Glee*), anything loud or lyric-intensive can be a distraction when reading. If you're really craving some white noise, DePorter suggests playing classical music softly in the background. (You're less likely to start singing along to a Baroque piece than you are to anything Taylor Swift/Pink/Beyonce-related.)

Chapter 10: Study Habits of the Rich and Famous (or at Least Academically Successful)

5. Studying with other people around
If your study session involves more girl talk than getting things done, you may want to rethink your study strategy. It's all about discipline. Working with a friend can be a fun way to review and memorize information—but you have to buckle down and do the work.

DePorter suggests studying with a friend and relating the topic you're working on to something you already know or like to up the studying fun factor. "When you know something well, you almost always find it interesting," she said.

If you'll only crack a book when there's something in the background to distract you, it may be a sign that you're really trying to put off studying altogether.

How prone you are to study procrastination may depend on how you feel about the class—or school itself. In many cases, students' relationships with their teachers can be a big factor.

"Some teachers are great at encouraging their students to take a deeper interest in their work," Shilpa R. Taufique, PhD said. "[It] also depends on how much parents take an interest in their teen's schoolwork."

In the end, studying all comes down to you—and how much time and effort you're willing to put in to be successful. Studying sometimes feels like work. But the pay-off (awesome grades, academic self-esteem, a general feeling of accomplishment and awe-inspiring brilliance) is worth the effort.

Quick Study Tips That Will Shrink Your Homework Time

You don't necessarily need to study more—you just need to study smarter.

DePorter's nine Quantum Learning tips may help you rock your next study session (or class, or test, or generally any kind of learning you next attempt to do):

1. S.L.A.N.T.: A system (and acronym) that can help you position yourself to perform better in class—literally.

Sit in the front row or middle section of the classroom. (No hiding in the back to zone out.)

Lean slightly forward in your chair, as if you are hanging on the teacher's every word. (Even if you aren't. Pretend.)

Chapter 10: Study Habits of the Rich and Famous (or at Least Academically Successful)

Ask questions to clarify anything you don't understand.

Nod your head to show you are listening and interested. (Note: Do this in moderation. You don't want your teacher to think you are rocking out to some music she can't hear and/or having a violent allergic reaction to something you ate earlier.)

Talk to your teacher after class to build rapport and establish a relationship. (This doesn't mean you have to suck up to your teacher. We're not taking about bringing in handmade gifts or exiting class by screaming, "THANK YOU!" and doing a cartwheel into the hall. Just be friendly—like you would with anyone else in the class. Say hi, say goodbye, ask about assignments.)

2. Use Test-Taking Strategies: DePorter suggests allowing enough time to get to class a few minutes early. (As someone who is chronically 5-10 minutes late, I'd suggest this, too. If you tend to be late, allow more time than you think will be necessary to get to class—and you'll probably get there right on time.) Hurrying causes tension, and you can use the few extra minutes to review your notes one last time.

Before and during the test, give yourself positive messages, like *I know this information and I'm going to get an A*. (Silently. Teachers tend to frown upon shouting out "I AM ROCKING THIS BAD BOY" in the middle of a test.)

If you feel yourself getting tense, close your eyes for a moment (just a moment—actually falling asleep would be bad) and take a few deep breaths. Imagine a relaxing scene. If you're having trouble concentrating or are feeling overwhelmed, try jotting down some notes in the margin of your paper to help you remember what you studied.

3. Create an Optimal Study Area: Designate a study area at home. Your homework haven should include a desk or table, a comfortable chair, and good lighting. For additional inspiration, you could add posters with positive messages printed on them (or adorable kittens dangling from a tree, reminding you to "hang in there).

When studying, always tackle the most difficult subjects first. Once you get them out of the way, the rest will seem that much easier.

4. Cultivate a Winning Attitude: Maintaining a positive attitude is your most important learning asset. Solid mental preparation is crucial before beginning any learning experience.

5. Remember, the "F" Stands for "Feedback": True, it also stands for "fail," as in "you just failed this assignment," and "for your

Chapter 10: Study Habits of the Rich and Famous (or at Least Academically Successful)

information, your parents are not going to be happy about it, so you can kiss your weekend plans goodbye." However, it's a basic truth that people—from infancy through adulthood—learn through mistakes. Remember to learn from the feedback you get from others, whether it is a failed test or a poor relationship. In your path to become an excellent learner, consider feedback valuable information that you need to succeed. And you will succeed—chock that F up to a lesson and turn it around before your next test.

6. Plan Ahead: Use a calendar to mark test days or due dates of important papers. Procrastination, while tempting, is the easy way out—and it doesn't do you any favors tension-wise. Studying ahead reduces stress and increases your ability to recall information at test time.

7. Discover the Power of "This is it!": "This is it!" means making the most of every moment. It also means doing whatever it takes to make a subject interesting. Don't waste time complaining—buckle down and tell yourself what you're learning is interesting and important. Use your powers of persuasion to get yourself psyched about the task at hand.

8. Overcome the Obstacle of a Blank Page with Free Writing: When faced with writer's block, free writing provides visible and immediate progress.

Choose a subject—any subject (it doesn't have to be about what you're working on). Set the timer for 5, 10, or 15 minutes (or really, any time you choose). Write continuously until your time is up. Don't worry about structuring sentences, checking grammar, backtracking, or crossing things out. The point isn't to write the best thing you possibly can—it's just to write. Free writing clears your mind, focuses your ideas, and makes the invisible visible.

9. Take Breaks: Take a short five-minute break for every 30 minutes of studying (which is much more effective than taking a 30-minute break for every five minutes of studying). In addition, whenever you notice your mind wandering, take a mini-break by standing up, stretching, and walking around a bit. You'll come back to your work more focused and refreshed.

Avoiding Procrastination (and Stress)

Having stellar study habits doesn't just help you ace tests and score great grades on written assignments—it can also help you reduce stress.

To help create a stress-free environment when studying, Christine Louise Hohlbaum, suggests storing all study supplies in one place to make life easier. "There's nothing worse than spending your precious time hunting stuff down," she said. "Designate a study-only area in your room [that is] gadget free!"

When you're through studying for a test or working on a big project, you should always reward yourself for a job well done.

Chapter 10: Study Habits of the Rich and Famous (or at Least Academically Successful)

"We know it can be tough, cramming for exams or working on that boring science project," Hohlbaum said. "Set milestones for yourself with the promise of a reward for each one you meet."

It may also help to ask yourself exactly why you're so prone to putting off studying. Are there just other things you'd rather do—or is there another reason?

"When there is a great deal of procrastination, I usually find some underlying insecurities or a lack of vision about their future—kind of a 'what's the point?' attitude," Shilpa R. Taufique, PhD said.

Taufique says she usually addresses procrastination issues by looking for those underlying factors and by helping individuals identify their short- and long-term goals. Then, the next step is to build excitement and enthusiasm about those goals.

So put procrastination in a drawer. And not one you open often, like your sock drawer. With focus and a clear goal in mind, there is nothing you can't do! (Except possibly have a sock drawer where all the socks actually match. That is a physical impossibility.)

Overcommitting

Overcommitting isn't always just a time management problem. According to Julius Licata, director of TeenCentral.Net at KidsPeace, a packed schedule can also be a sign that someone is trying to carve out an identity.

"Teens are looking for success, but even more, they are looking for acceptance," Licata said. "They feel they have to work harder to achieve the kind of success they seek. "They [can] feel 'maxed out' and don't know how to reel it in. Parents are often unaware of this because of their own schedules, which leaves little time for family and support."

Of course, fitting in isn't the only reason we do the things we do. But sometimes you need to take a step back and realize just how much stress you put yourself under with everything you do. Just remember, it's okay to say "no" every once in a while. Your body will thank you (not necessarily with a note, but with a general feeling of happiness instead of exhaustion).

Set limits on your activity time—and schedule some leisure time. Having personal time for just you is key. That means turning off the computer, silencing the cell phone, and just enjoying being by yourself.

Your "me time" doesn't have to be anything major. Pick up a book, or your journal, or sketch for a while. Whatever you feel like doing (even sleeping counts. Really. That's the great thing about me time—it's totally your call.)

Chapter 11:
SETTING (AND REACHING) GOALS

Chapter 11: Setting (and Reaching) Goals

If you've ever made a New Year's resolution, you've set a goal.

And you probably know, based on whether or not you kept that resolution, that following through to reach a goal takes both planning and work.

Setting your goal, deciding which habit or aspect of your life you want to change is the easiest part. As a result, many people don't fully follow through on those New Year's resolutions.

According to a recent *Miami Herald* article, 40-45 percent of people make resolutions on New Year's Day. Yet almost 97 percent of their resolutions—um, which is basically all of them—of their resolutions for the year don't ever come to fruition.

So kudos to those people who achieve three percent of their resolutions: That is work well done! Part of the problem? Sticking to your plan to make a change. When it comes to New Year's resolutions, 75 percent of people who make them will adhere to that resolution for at least a week; 46 percent will keep a resolution mindset through six months, according to the *Herald*.

Clearly, it helps to make a solid resolution—and put your plan in motion fast. A good goal is one that's made and executed with planning and attention.

So why should you set goals at all? Because reaching them—and even working to reach them—can help you learn and feel good about yourself.

"Time can seem like it goes on forever," Shilpa R. Taufique, PhD said. "Building in goals and objectives that can be realistically attained in shorter periods of time can serve to build confidence."

Setting Goals: How to Get There, Step by Step

Setting goals can help you achieve an unparalleled sense of accomplishment and improve different aspects of your life.

Chapter 11: Setting (and Reaching) Goals

Never set a single goal? Read on to find out how to decide what to do—and how to do it.

Decide on an objective. What would you like to change? Do you want to be healthier? Why not try to eat less processed foods or drink more water? Are you chronically late? Aim to be on-time everywhere you go for a week. Whatever your goals are, try tackling one thing at a time to start.

Establish a plan to do it. Whether it involves reading a book, getting advice, creating a schedule, or something else entirely, make sure you have a method to tackle your goal over time.

Set a general deadline. Pick a date by which you'd like to see some definitive changes. It will help encourage you to get started and stay on track.

Kick-start your success. Once you have a plan, set it in motion right away—before you lose any of your overflowing enthusiasm.

Determine a reward. Hard work deserves a celebration—and having a reward or treat planned for when you reach your goal can help you stay on track.

Trying to get more sleep? Consider splurging on new PJs when you make it through a month of getting eight hours a night.

Hoping to speed up your per-mile pace so you'll be in great shape for the spring track season? Giving yourself a few days off running once you reach your time. All that improvement could inspire you to keep training right up until the season starts.

And don't beat yourself up too badly about any roadblocks you encounter. Along the way to your goal, if you have a bad day—or week—and find yourself a little off course, focus on the big picture. Think about all the positive stuff you've already achieved.

Remember: Every day is a new chance for health, happiness—and all those other good things.

"While focusing on future goals is important, I always emphasize the importance of being present in the moment," Taufique said. "All of us, especially teens, can get caught up in what went wrong in the past and what we want or don't want in the future."

Remember that the past is the past—and focus on how much better you're making your life today by making positive changes.

"We can't really do much about those things [in the past], but we can make the present moment the best it can be," Taufique said.

Chapter 11: Setting (and Reaching) Goals

Your Foolproof Goal-Setting Worksheet

Keeping regular tabs on how you're doing with your goal can help you stay on course. Use our foolproof worksheet for laying out—and sticking to—your goal. (For example, my goal was to create a foolproof worksheet for laying out and sticking to goals. And look! I did! It works!)

MY GOAL:

_____

GENERAL DEADLINE:

_____

WHY I WANT TO DO THIS:

_____

_____

_____

HOW I'M GOING TO GET THERE:

_____

REWARD WHEN I REACH MY GOAL:

_____

HALFWAY POINT CHECK-IN

WHAT PROGRESS HAS BEEN MADE?

_____

THE GOAL IS STILL IMPORTANT TO ME BECAUSE …

_____

WAYS I PLAN TO KEEP ON TRACK:

_____

_____

_____

Conclusion: It's Good to Be a Girl

Now that you've learned how to have the perfect social life; utilize killer study habits; be uber-confident; be more nutritious; set goals; and *throw* the ultimate party, you're ready to master the next few years of your life. (Or at least be really healthy, social and ambitious until college. Which works, too.)

Your only job right now is to stay positive, focused and happy—and relax and enjoy the ride.

A lot happens during junior high and high school. You learn a lot about what you like and don't like; you learn a lot about your friends—and you learn a ton about yourself.

You'll most likely try on a few new personalities or take on a few new personality traits; some you may keep, others you'll ditch. You're going to have some crazy new experiences; you'll probably stumble across some regrets, too. Don't beat yourself up too much when you do. That learning process will continue for the rest of your life—so don't worry if there are a few slip-ups or bumps along the way.

Just remember that you're already awesome.

And as you learn more things—and work to grow, treat others well and educate yourself on everything from history to walking in high heels (during which everyone is entitled to at least one big shoe wipeout, so if you wobble a little, don't worry)—you're going to become *even more awesome*. (I promise.)

So get out there, get active—and start having fun.

(Just not so much that you max out your schedule. Or get super stressed. Or can't fit in at least seven hours sleep a night. You get the idea.)

Good luck on all the unbelievably amazing adventures you're going to have! You are undoubtedly in for a wild ride. I can't promise it'll all be super easy (in fact, I can almost guarantee parts of it won't be), but I can tell you this: your teen years will be, without question, a unique, exciting experience—and I hope you enjoy every single exhilarating, enlightening, awe-inspiring moment.

About the Author

Erin Brereton is a freelance writer and editor who lives in Chicago. The author of several nonfiction books on teen celebrities, tech gadgets, and other topics, Brereton previously worked as senior editor on *mary-kateandashley* magazine and has also has written and reported for the *Chicago Tribune, Life & Style Weekly, Legal Management*, CommonSenseMedia.org, and other publications.

Brereton is a graduate of Northwestern University's Medill School of Journalism and the Second City comedy writing program (guess which one had funnier homework?) and has volunteered for a number of teen-based organizations, including Jobs for Youth. In addition, Brereton was once a teenage girl—who possessed little to no mastery of nutrition, scheduling, and many of the other topics covered in this book.